When Truth Knocks

Eddie D. Fleming

BookLocker
Trenton, Georgia

Paperback ISBN: 978-1-64719-930-2
Hardcover ISBN: 978-1-64719-931-9
Ebook ISBN: 978-1-64719-932-6

Published by BookLocker.com, Inc., Trenton, Georgia.

Printed on acid-free paper.

BookLocker.com, Inc.
2022

First Edition

This book is dedicated to my wife, Laura, and my two children, Elizabeth, and Evan, who have put up with my procrastination and chaotic writing schedule in producing this book.

And a big thank you to Concord General Baptist Church for taking a chance on me 30 years ago in choosing me as their pastor.

When Truth Knocks
A Journey Through Life's Spiritual Fog

Eddie D. Fleming

Contents

Introduction 1

Chapter 1: The Journey Begins 5

Chapter 2: The Deceptions Along the Way 11

Chapter 3: The Shortcuts to Avoid 37

Chapter 4: The Counterfeit Salvation 53

Chapter 5: The Self-Examination 65

Chapter 6: The Right Path 75

Chapter 7: The Essentials 89

Chapter 8: The Spiritual Benefits 103

Chapter 9: The Spiritual Effects 127

Chapter 10: The Visible Evidence 151

Chapter 11: The Precious Promises 167

Conclusion 185

Endnotes 189

Introduction

The fear of truth by some, the rejection of truth by others, and the perversion of truth by many reveal the power and importance of truth. The primary role truth plays in our lives, our society, and our future is undeniable. Truth can ease our conscience and lower our blood pressure. It can protect the innocent and set free the falsely imprisoned. Jesus once said, "...the truth will set you free" (John 8:32).

Unfortunately, much pain and sorrow are inflicted daily on those who reject, ignore, and run from the truth. Marriages are destroyed, businesses fail, careers are decimated, and lives are lost because truth is rejected or perverted. A stranger helped me grasp the significance of ignoring truth.

I was all along in my church when I was startled by a loud pounding at the front door. The man's breaking voice and watery eyes said it all. He was looking for help, hope, and a place to hide. He sought the nearest church because that's what churches do; they help people or are supposed to.

I don't remember his name, but I do his pain. He was hurting. He was desperate. He was seeking someone, anyone who could give him a glimmer of hope. His greatest fear was in his driveway. It was a deputy sheriff's car. He knew what awaited him. The divorce papers would end his marriage, and he wasn't ready to accept them. Therefore, he bolted and found himself in my office.

The scene was the ultimate act of ignored truths, overlooked telltale signs, and a refusal to face reality. The man's marriage didn't have to end this way. According to him, he had seen the signs, heard the warnings, but refused to acknowledge and act on them. He now is plagued with the "if onlys."

Why didn't he listen? Why not heed his wife's warnings, attend to her needs, and respond to her pleas? Why? Why do we not act on truths that can save our marriage? Why don't we listen to our physicians and medical experts? Why don't we listen to the God who loves us, the Savior who died for us, and the Holy Spirit who wants to guide us?

This book seeks to answer such questions. It's a book about truth, precisely spiritual truths that I've discovered on my spiritual journey. Its contents can help protect us from evil and bless us with good. It can enable us to navigate the spiritual fog of today, and in the end, allow us to enjoy the life God has given us and obtain the eternal life God wants for us. The truths I've learned can help you avoid the mistakes I've made and the wrong conclusions I've embraced.

Of course, for the truth to change us, to liberate us, we must do more than just know it. We have to understand it and act on it. We have to accept the ugly truth about ourselves, the frightening truths about our enemies, and the beautiful truths about God. We also have to understand what's behind our fear and rejection of truth. It is more than the baggage of our past and the stubbornness of our hearts. There is a real and present enemy among us. There are spiritual powers of wickedness in high places (see Ephesians 6:12). In the beginning, Eve rejected the truth of God because she listened to the enemy of God. This scenario plays out every day and in every part of the world.

Knowing the truth about the enemy of humanity is a necessity. But, first, we need to understand how he works. We need to know that he hasn't changed; deception is still his game. We need to see that broken marriages, devastated families, divided churches, ruined lives, and nations in chaos are in his shadow. We need to know that Satan is the father of lies, the accuser of the saints, and the deceiver of the world. We need to know that if he can't get the lost to reject God, he will convince them they already have God. If he can't convince Christians to abandon God, he will try to convince them God has abandoned them.

The man in my office was a product of Satan's handiwork. His marriage was in shambles and his life in disarray. After an hour or so, he left my office and headed home to face the truth. If only I could have given him a kernel of truth or a nugget of wisdom that would have fixed his marriage and healed his heart, but I had neither. Truth in hindsight can't undo our past, but it can help shape our future. Beyond a little comfort, and a prayer, I could do little to help him. But what I can do is warn others about the enemy, and most of all, share the truths that can guide us, protect us, encourage us, comfort us, liberate us, and save us. But, of course, truth can only knock; we must let it in. We must receive it, believe it, and act on it.

Chapter 1:
The Journey Begins

All journeys involve risks. I have traveled to the other side of the world and back safely. But, then experienced a $2,000 plus accident while still partially in my driveway (Don't ask, it's not one of my fonder memories). So the risks are real, but as with mountain climbing, the greater the risk, the bigger the reward.

My journey has been long and sometimes difficult. I began, as do most, without a plan in hand. I simply traveled with an awareness of the big picture and a willingness to examine, seek, and be open to truth along the way. I realize many factors have contributed to my spiritual liberation.

One factor was being aware of the fantastic world in which we live. The beauty of a rainbow, a majestic mountaintop covered with new-fallen snow, or the landscape transformed into breathtaking scenes filled with vivid fall colors dancing in the wind. These wonders couldn't just happen by chance. How could there not be a creator, a Great Designer behind it all? I later discovered Psalm 19:1, "The heavens declare the glory of God, and the sky above proclaims his handiwork."

Along the way, I have contemplated a world without God and found it wanting. I noted conversations with believers and non-believers. I examined proposed truths by opponents and proponents of religion. I listened to valid points, rejecting those without merit. My journey, as with most, included bumps,

> However, unlike the fogs of August, spiritual fogs do not dissipate on their own. If the truth doesn't come knocking, we must ask, seek, and knock in search of it.

wrong turns, unmarked highways, and fog, lots of fog. Oh, I hate fog.

Spiritual journeys must contend with fog. If you've ever driven through dense fog, you know what it's like. Finding your destination is difficult. Visibility is restricted. Landmarks and reference points become almost invisible. Stop signs and traffic signals become useless. Missed turns and deadly crashes often occur. However, unlike the fogs of August, spiritual fogs do not dissipate on their own. If the truth doesn't come knocking, we must ask, seek, and knock in search of it.

Spiritual fog can produce wrong beliefs, decisions based on deception, and spiritual causalities. I know, for I have been there. I know what it is like to have your mind confused and cluttered by the spiritual hodgepodge that pollutes our country, dominates our airwaves, and fills our bookstores.

However, fog or no fog, the road most taken in life is traveled searching for truth, spiritual truth. As long as humanity has existed, it has sought the truth about God, tried to please God, and worshipped a form of God. In ancient times, belief in God or gods helped explain many natural phenomena. However, in our modern, enlightened, and knowledge-filled world, the human mind still believes in God. We want to know what He's like, what He wants, and how to know Him. But why is this true? It's in our programming. God has created us for a relationship with Him. The absence of this relationship leaves an emptiness in us that needs filling. French mathematician and philosopher Blaise Pascal wrote:

> What else does this craving, and this helplessness, proclaim but that there was once in man a true happiness, of which all that now remains is the empty print and trace? This he tries in vain to fill with everything around him, seeking in things that are not there the help he cannot find in those that are, though none can help, since this infinite abyss can be filled only with an infinite and immutable object; in other words by God himself.
> - Blaise Pascal, Pensées VII (425).

Our conscious and unconscious need for meaning and purpose in life is symptomatic of this emptiness that can only be fully satisfied by knowing God personally.

This hunger for God drives us to search for spiritual truth, but such a search involves risk and danger. We put at risk our cherished beliefs. We may be forced out of our comfortable *status quo*. In the end, it could cost us our friends, our families, and in some parts of the world, our lives.

Jesus warned us. He said that those who embark on such a journey must be prepared to make sacrifices.

And a scribe came up and said to him, 'Teacher,
I will follow you wherever you go.' 20And Jesus
said to him, 'Foxes have holes, and birds of the
air have nests, but the Son of Man has nowhere
to lay his head. (Matthew 8:19-20)

In John's gospel, Jesus said:

If you were of the world, the world would love
you as its own; but because you are not of the
world, but I chose you out of the world, therefore
the world hates you. 20 Remember the word that
I said to you: 'A servant is not greater than his
master.' If they persecuted me, they will also
persecute you. (John 15:19–20)

The journey for truth will always involve risks. Risks can
be frightening. Discovered truths can turn your world upside
down. They can bring sorrow and pain to you and your loved
ones. As a result, some hesitate, procrastinate, or abandon the
journey altogether. However, the best decision we can ever
make is to pursue truth. Why? Because the risks and the

> Our choices determine the people we become, the
> deeds we do, and the future we create. Therefore,
> we must choose wisely, which means making
> choices based on knowledge.

hardships are not worthy of being compared to the rewards of a journey well-traveled and new truths joyfully received.

Of course, any journey requires making choices. Our choices determine the people we become, the deeds we do, and the future we create. Therefore, we must choose wisely, making choices based on knowledge. We must seek the knowledge we need.

In my search for information, I discovered a world of surprises. There is no limit to the various ideas about God, hell, heaven, and other spiritual matters. Yes, the fog is dense in the spiritual realm. Therefore, we can expect significant disagreement about who God is, how we can know God, the pathway to God, and whether heaven or hell even exists. Therefore, handle with care those you meet along the way and the supposed truths they share. Remember, they, too, are searching. They, too, may be in the dark but believe they are in the light. None of us have a lock on truth. We all need to grow in our knowledge of God and, hopefully, our relationship with God.

The one constant in journeys is that they often include the unexpected; this was true for me. As my understanding of God grew, my view of others changed. I came to realize more fully our equality. Therefore, we have no reason to look down on others, nor should we fear them (at least not because they believe differently than us). On the one hand, we have no motive for hostility, for we are in the same fog.

On the other hand, we are all made in God's image. Therefore, let our commonality be a foundation for knowing and loving one another. One of the great teachings of

Christianity is the call to love others, even those we might consider our enemies.

God has given us a diverse world that should be a land of learning instead of a battlefield for divisiveness. Although differences will create demarcation lines, the lines can be picket fences, where conversations can occur between opposing sides instead of concrete and barbed-wire barriers. The choice is yours. I hope you will embrace the journey by going to the next chapter.

Chapter 2:
The Deceptions Along the Way

Life's journey would be one big joy ride if we could believe all that we hear, trust the people we meet, and count on the promises they make, but we can't. Just as insects dot our windshields, lies litter our journey. Therefore, we can expect to encounter lies and liars along our way. Lies will be disguised as truths or half-truths, and the deceivers may be delightful on the outside but deadly on the inside. The master deceiver, the Devil, never tires of deceiving the multitudes and shaming the saints. He seeks both the young and the old. No aspect of life is safe from him. He pollutes our political landscape, bombards our business world, contaminates the church, and causes chaos in the lives of Christians. The world is comprised of two kinds of people, those seeking to deceive and those targeted for deception.

The Bible states, "We know that we are children of God and that the whole world is under the control of the evil one" (1 John 5:19). Only the children of God can be free of the Devil's power and manipulation. If we are not a child of God, we are pawns of Satan. He uses and abuses all of humanity. He uses those under his spell to practice his deceptive devices and demonic appeals. We find his efforts everywhere; in books, commercials, and political speeches. Every day, both young and old, buy into his scams, schemes, and seditions promoted by con artists, amoral public figures, special interest groups, charismatic personalities, as well as the philosophies and ideologies of street gangs, terrorist groups, educators, politicians, and dubious religious leaders.

Who has not been his victim? Who has not been duped and tricked by the unscrupulous? Who has not bought into the delight of deception only to suffer at the hands of the destroyer?

What's scary is you, I, or anyone, can embrace deception without knowing it. So we must be alert to the Devil's methods and mission. His mission is to steal, kill, and destroy (John 10:10a). He hates God and everything connected to God. He is powerless to hurt God; therefore, he comes after the people of God and the creation of God. His plan is simple: deceive the world about death, the Devil, and the divine. Amazingly, it is working. Many believe all roads lead to heaven, or there is no heaven to go to and no hell from which to run. A growing number believe there is no God to turn to and no Satan to avoid.

Of course, the best way to defend against the master deceiver is to be aware of his presence, practice, and people. Therefore, we must be alert at all times. And when he knocks on your door and tries to invade your life, just say no. Resist the Devil, and he will flee from you. Instead, look to Christ, and He will strengthen you. The Bible puts it this way, "Submit yourselves therefore to God. Resist the devil, and he will flee from you" (James 4:7).

Deceivers

Satan will not show up dressed in a red suit with a tail and pitchfork. He will be the buyer on the internet, the other person in the chat room, or the boyfriend or girlfriend that tries to seduce you. Even as I write this book, I find myself inundated with deceivers roaming the internet. I had placed my used refrigerator on Craigslist for sale when I quickly received, not one, or two, or even three, but four offers to buy it and pay an extra $40, and in one case $50 if I would hold it until the buyer gets the money to me. So, I agreed. I sent the lucky buyer the information he needed, my name and address, so he could send me a cashier's check. However, later that day, he notified me that his PA (personal assistant) had put my name on the check meant for the movers and sent it to me. He asked if I would cash the check and then send him the amount exceeding my portion of the check. His request threw up a red flag for me, not to mention that a person who has a personal assistant is buying a used refrigerator off the internet. (Note: Red flags are essential in both the physical and spiritual realms.) So, I searched on the internet for frauds connected to Craigslist. I discovered that scammers often send fake cashier checks or money orders that exceed the designated amount. Then they ask you to wire them the amount in excess. A few days later, you are left holding the preverbal bag after the bank finds out the check or money order is fake. You are required to reimburse the bank for the complete cashier's check and any charges attached to it.

Although I changed my ad to include *CASH ONLY* and am *not interested in dealing with out-of-state scammers,* they continued to contact me. The deceivers of this world are relentless when it involves financial gain or spiritual sedition.

The phrase may be old, but it's still relevant. "When something sounds too good to be true, it probably is too good to be true." The same is true of spiritual leaders who promise

> In the beginning, Satan used a tree and a lie to deceive Eve, but throughout the ages, he has simply used people who tell lies.

health, wealth, and divine protection from all the earthly pain and suffering of a sin-cursed world. When their mouths are moving, and the red flags are flapping, look to the Scriptures. When the promises proclaimed by people go beyond the promises declared by God, listen to God, and reject the others.

In the beginning, Satan used a tree and a lie to deceive Eve, but throughout the ages, he has simply used people who tell lies. History is littered with religious leaders who have mastered the technique of deception. Jim Jones, who led his group of followers to the jungle of Guyana, is a good example. His silver tongue promoted a social gospel that was nothing more than socialism wrapped in religious garb. He deceived politicians, news media outlets, and thousands of followers. In the end, his deception led to over 900 suicides at Jonestown in Guyana on November 18, 1978.

Why was he able to deceive mayors, presidential candidates, and many news outlets? Because we yearn for that perfect world, which Mr. Jones was supposedly establishing. God created us in His image. He made us for an ideal world, but sin corrupted it. Therefore, we long for a world free of disease, poverty, racism, prejudice, and violence. However, this very desire for a utopian world makes us gullible and susceptible to masters of deceit like Jim Jones.

This desire is also why we are so open to prosperity gospel preaching. We all want the ravages of sin eradicated from our world. However, the answer to a sin-plagued world is not a health and wealth philosophy but a heavenly home free of sin, Satan, and sorrows.

Any religious leader whose teachings contradict the Word of God is ignorant of the truth or bent on deceiving others about the truth. Either way, they are dangerous and deserve to be rejected and removed from places of leadership and positions of influence.

However, it's not just cult leaders who dabble in deception. Organized church has had its dark moments. On March 15, 1517, Pope Leo X needed money to rebuild St. Peter's Basilica, so he granted indulgences to those who donated to its reconstruction. Johann Tetzel, a middle-aged Dominican friar, became the Pope's primary marketer of indulgences. Robert J. Morgan writes, Mr. Tetzel traveled throughout Europe like P. T. Barnum, with "a bag of printed receipts.... (declaring) I have here the passports to lead the human soul to the celestial joys of Paradise." [1]

Who doesn't want their friends and loved ones to dwell with them in a pain-free, joy-filled, eternal home? Who doesn't long for a perfect world? Well, guess what? The enemy knows it. His deceit masters target us. False teachers shower us with their empty promises and error-filled philosophies—tapping into our minds, emotions, and money.

Satan is very inclusive. He targets everyone. He seeks to divide, destroy, and deceive anyone and everyone. (Are we not seeing this in our world?) If given a door of opportunity, he will enter. He never ceases in his attempts to infiltrate denominations, churches, and even the hearts and minds of believers. Sadly, we are all too familiar with his deception and deceit. Our personal histories contain the names and faces of people Satan has used to inflict

> Unfortunately, as long as the world exists, there will be deceivers, seeking to deceive and enslave us.

his deception on us, although unknown to the world.

Unfortunately, when the dust settles, the victims' stories are all too familiar. In the end, the deceived face an obvious truth. The end is always diametrically opposite of its beginning. In the beginning, we delight in it. When we see our dream coming true, our desire being fulfilled, or our hope materializing, we rejoice in it. (Eve thought she would be like God.) But, of course, we didn't have a clue what was happening. We may have had a gut feeling something wasn't right. Still, we did not know that the deceiver was pulling the wool over our eyes. Sadly, we would learn soon enough that the pot of gold we were chasing, or the false hope we were embracing, would turn into a tempest of trouble and a lot of loss.

Unfortunately, as long as this world exists, there will be deceivers seeking to deceive and enslave us. I know. They have deceived me many times, including spiritually. As a result, I was spiritually lost while living under a cloud of deception. I was singing the songs of the gospel but denying the state of my soul. I was firmly connected to the church but disconnected from God.

However, during my childhood, my family didn't attend church. Still, we did operate under Christian principles and embraced the Christian mindset. We watched Billy Graham on television and had a big family Bible on the tea table (stuffed with paper clippings). But the church was not for us, bible study was not our thing, and prayer was what we did in times of desperation.

The climax of my deception occurred during my childhood. My brother and I attended a tent crusade with a friend and her dad. At the conclusion of the service, my response insulated me from God by cunningly convincing me I had God.

The Bible calls Satan the master deceiver (See 2 John 7 & Revelation 12:9). Sadly, he worked his magic on me. Almost eight years later, I realized I had embraced a counterfeit conversion. (More about this later.)

Unfortunately, society is increasingly succumbing to Satan's deceptions. Churches and whole denominations have embraced the world's philosophies on gender and sexuality and rejected the Bible. Hank Hanegraaff puts it well in his book *Christianity In Crisis.* He points out that many who claim to be Christians have embraced a distorted view of Christianity in recent times. As a result, millions reject true Christianity because of the false version others have adopted and promoted as authentic Christianity. He then points out that under the label of "Jesus is Lord," many are being tricked into embracing a religion of greed while adhering to metaphysical teachings. And, worse of all, they believe their counterfeit Christianity is the real thing. He further warns that Christianity is speeding into a "crisis of unparalleled proportions."[2]

Jesus may have fed the multitudes with fish and bread, but today Satan feeds them with lies, half-truths, and false beliefs. He and his spiritual shysters actively seek to deceive the world about the Christian faith, life after death, and the reality of God. Therefore, there is a great need for truth. Truth is Satan's kryptonite. Wherever truth lives, his deceit dies. However, embracing the truth is just the beginning. Afterward, we must continually live in the truth and stay on guard against those who oppose the truth.

Unfortunately, finding the path to truth is difficult in a world filled with the fog of deception. Have you ever wondered why deception is so prevalent in our world? Why are we so easily deceived? Why do sane people believe they will win the lottery's jackpot or a 100-million-dollar sweepstake despite years of evidence to the contrary and odds that are astronomical? The answer has to do with the desire within.

Desire Within

When we become discontent with reality, we open ourselves up to fantasy and deception—all kinds of deception. Thus, when our back is against the wall, an offer of help catches our eye, and Satan knows it and takes advantage of it.

> The desire within deactivates our warning systems and paves the way for deceivers to enter.

This kind of deception happened to one of my church members years ago. He called, seeking my help. He asked that I write his verbal instructions on what would be done with his possessions after his passing. First, he allocated $500,000 to the Billy Graham Association. Then $1,000.000 to the Red Cross. Finally, another $500,000 to our church. I was confused—he had very few worldly possessions. Therefore, before he could give away another million, I interrupted him. "Hold on a minute," I said. "How did you come across this money?" "I won it," he replied. "How and from whom did you win it?" I asked. Although he couldn't give me any specifics, I got enough out of him to realize it had to do with a sweepstake. It was then I put it all together. I had recently received a Publisher's Clearing House Sweepstakes envelope in the mail. I also remembered when my dad mistakenly thought he had won the same sweepstake.

When I tried to prepare him for the likelihood that he didn't win it, he was adamant he had indeed won it. I then asked if I could visit him. Which he was eager for me to do. Sure enough, the wording of the sweepstakes' notification seemed to show he had won it, but on close examination, he had won nothing. So,

> But each person is tempted when he is lured and enticed by his own desire. 15 Then desire when it has conceived gives birth to sin, and sin when it is fully grown brings forth death. (James 1:14-15)

unfortunately, I became the bearer of a painful, dream-crushing truth. After he sadly accepted the fact, he shared the financial pit he and his son had dug for him. He had a phone bill that was in the thousands of dollars. He said, "I needed to win this sweepstake."

The Bible says:

> But each person is tempted when he is lured and enticed by his own desire. 15 Then desire when it has conceived gives birth to sin, and sin when it is fully grown brings forth death. (James 1:14-15)

A person dying of thirst in the desert is susceptible to the mental deception known as a mirage. A person in deep debt is ripe for the shyster offering quick financial gains. People who are empty spiritually are ready to soak up any belief system that comes along, regardless of its validity. The desire within deactivates our warning systems and paves the way for deceivers to enter.

However, some deceptions don't require specialized promoters; they occur naturally. Family beliefs are typically passed down to the next generation, whether valid or false. The same is true in organized religion. New members readily receive false doctrines. Established members close their minds to any challenges to their doctrines.

Thus, we must face a quandary. How can we determine if our belief system or doctrine is false? It's difficult, but thankfully, not impossible. Like some Olympic events, deception carries a high level of difficulty. It is hard to recognize one's involvement in the deception. The deceived are blinded from the truth and convinced they have the truth. When we are sure of something, we close our minds to opposing views and differing opinions.

For instance, many believe in God, not because of the evidence, but the desire they feel. The opposite is also true. Some don't believe in God, but it has nothing to do with evidence but with their desire. They don't want to believe in God.

The temptation is to embrace deception to avoid painful truths. And, unfortunately, human nature wants to take the broad way. We like living in a comfort zone.

Comfort Zone

Many would rather live with a comfortable lie than face a painful truth. Therefore, many will sacrifice truth at the altar of comfort. By embracing deception, we can hear what we want to hear, see what we want to see, and believe what we want to believe.

But, even as we sacrifice truth for comfort, we sense something isn't right deep down. However, the delusion we're living under feels too good to turn loose. As long as our erroneous belief is a comfortable fit, why change? Why rock the boat?

After one of my son's baseball training sessions, he shared a quote that his trainer had shared with him. "The comfort zone is a beautiful place, but nothing ever grows there." The author is anonymous, but its truth is timeless. If we grow mentally, physically, and spiritually, we must get out of our comfort zone. (The Pharisees refused to do so.)

In the early stages of my Christian faith, my beliefs and understanding of the Bible came mainly from the teachings of ministers, Sunday school teachers, and other Christians. For a short time, I was comfortable with those beliefs.

However, the more time I spent in the Bible and exposed myself to various writings of Christian authors (trustworthy ones), I soon formed my own beliefs. Instead of just embracing the views of others. During this process, something unique happened. I began thinking for myself. As a result, I discovered that some of my beliefs didn't align with the truths of the Bible.

The Bible contains a multitude of truths and teachings. Some are clear and concise, contained in a verse or a paragraph. Others are woven throughout the Scriptures and are clarified by various verses and passages. When our biblical knowledge base grows, and we discover conflicts between what we believe and what the Bible teaches, we experience a conflict of conscience. We have a spiritual dilemma. When truth invades our comfort zone, we get uncomfortable. We are faced with a choice. Do we change our beliefs to accommodate the truth we have discovered? Do we ignore, deny, or excuse away the truth we have found; to accommodate our treasured belief (our deception)? Do we choose to remain in our comfort zone?

Change can be painful, not just for us, but for those associated with us—our family, friends, and fellow church members. Although many years have passed, I still remember the conversation like it was yesterday. I had visited a

> If we are people of truth, which people of faith must be, and everybody should be, we will be open to new truths, regardless of how painful they may be.

pastor friend just a few days before leaving for Bible College. The last thing he said to me as I entered my car was, *Don't let them change you.* I knew what he meant, don't let them liberalize you. But as I drove away, I thought, *Don't let them change you.* That was precisely the thing I wanted, of course, not in the way my friend was concerned. I understood that change is a part of growth. No change equals no growth. We cannot allow our fear of change to cause us to reject new truths, new knowledge, and new possibilities. We will miss a more fulfilling and spiritually enriching life if we do. We must be willing to leave our comfort zone.

If we are people of truth, which people of faith must be, and everybody should be, we will be open to new truths, regardless of how painful they may be. If we have been deceived or live with deception, we need to know it. We need to be free of it. I have experienced truth pain more than once. However, truth, not our love of comfort, or our dislike of pain, must be the basis for our decisions and beliefs.

The first significant shift in my understanding of God and His workings was painful. It occurred while I was attending a revival service at a nearby church. As was my custom, I was sitting on the front pew when the speaker approached the podium. However, when he opened his message folder, I was suddenly faced with a dilemma. Other Christians and ministers had warned me that a sermon, which was indeed from God, came spontaneously from the Holy Spirit as the minister yields himself to God. Therefore, prepared notes meant a non-spiritual and human-oriented message.

I suddenly found myself torn. If I stayed, I would condone, even showing approval of this unspiritual method of preaching, or so I thought. But, on the other hand, I would also go against my conscience and betray God. What should I do? It was now the midpoint of the service. The choir had finished singing, and the guest minister had begun speaking. I then thought, should I take a stand for truth and God by walking out, even though it meant walking past every pew on my way out. I was just about to leave when I remembered (that is, when the Holy Spirit reminded me) what a minister once told me. "Every person is made in the image of God; therefore, everybody, regardless of what we may think of them or their message, deserves to be treated with respect and dignity."

I reluctantly concluded that the minister deserved respect because he was created in God's image. My decision to stay was accompanied by silent prayer. *Dear God, help me get something out of this canned sermon.* And boy, did He! Although it's been over forty years since that day, I can still remember that his topic was on the love of God from the book of Hosea. As I listened, scales fell from my eyes. Light broke through the darkness of deception and ignorance. The sermon forever changed me, for the better.

In my attempt to honor God, I had dishonored Him. I had placed Him in a box. In my ignorance, and because of the falsehood I had embraced, I determined how God could and could not operate in a minister's life.

I had been deceived into believing that God, who is all-knowing, couldn't know what message the minister should preach until the minister stepped into the pulpit.

That night, on the front pew of a small country church, I learned a painful but eye-opening and mind-changing truth about sermon preparation. God's word later confirmed this truth. (I love it when God does this.) In John 14:16, 26, and 16:7, Jesus foretold of the coming of the Holy Spirit, referring to Him as the Helper (English Standard Version). In the original Greek language, the word for helper, *paracletos,* means the one who comes alongside and helps. It is not the Holy Spirit's job to provide prepackaged sermons. However, it is His job to assist ministers in preparing biblical messages. Furthermore, He is not limited. He can do it days, months, and even years in advance, for time has no meaning to God.

Life is full of painful truths we will experience on our spiritual journey. But with every deception we escape from, we move closer to being like the Jesus we love and nearer to

> Sadly, some choose to reject truth and embrace deception for the sake of comfort.

the heaven we desire. I am thankful for new truths and their role in adjusting my beliefs, correcting my convictions, and increasing my understanding of God.

What about you? Is your understanding of God deepening? Have your beliefs changed along the way? As we learn and grow in our knowledge of the Bible and God, our beliefs, convictions, and spiritual understanding will grow. Spiritual growth requires a willingness to abandon one's comfort zone. However, the comfort many enjoy may be more important than the truth they discover. When this happens, spiritual growth stops. Sadly, some choose to reject truth and embrace deception for the sake of comfort.

But not all truths are of equal magnitude; therefore, some are easy, and others are more difficult to accept. For instance, I had always heard and believed that chameleons can change colors to blend in with their surroundings, thus protecting themselves from would-be predators. It turns out they change their colors to reflect their emotional state. It has nothing to do with camouflage. It has nothing to do with self-preservation. Therefore, I readily accepted it because it didn't affect my comfort zone. It didn't require that I or those associated with me make any critical changes, which is not the case with new spiritual truths.

While people can't change their colors, they can change their beliefs, and often it has nothing to do with new knowledge or truth. Some do it not to reflect their emotions but to protect them. Emotions are given to us by God, but Satan has highjacked them. Emotions provide pleasure and motivate us to action. The purpose of our emotions is not to help us determine what steps we should take or whether an issue is right or wrong. Emotional discomfort, like its sister, physical pain, alerts us to a problem within us or around us. For instance, pain is our friend until we find out what is causing it. I know that the ER personnel will do nothing for your kidney stone pain until they determine it is a kidney stone issue. Although I'm an expert on kidney stones (over five stones make me an expert), they insist on tests to confirm it before they give me anything to relieve it.

A truth we don't like, a problem we must face, or a decision we must make can cause emotional discomfort. Unfortunately, emotionally immature people avoid dealing with issues, making tough decisions, and accepting disturbing truths. Instead, they seek a world that is emotionally safe from all discomfort. When they experience realities or statements that create unsettling emotions, they seek to ban or attack such issues without considering their merits. In doing so, they make their feelings lord of their lives. In doing so, they jettison any disturbing truth, fact, or reality into the trash heap of relativism and escapism.

Unfortunately, we all are creatures of comfort. Therefore, we must be on guard against the lure of the comfort zone. Examine your beliefs. Do they reflect the truths you have or the comforts you enjoy? For example, people raised in a family and community that believes in God would be comfortable believing in God; therefore, they will continue without biblical support. On the other hand, suppose one belongs to a family that does not believe in God. In that case, it is more comfortable to continue disbelieving in God, regardless of the evidence that contradicts one's nonbelief.

Could this help explain the exodus of young people from the church and the Christian faith after becoming involved in the culture of their secular university? For instance, a believer who moves to a nonbelieving community (increasingly, this is the case when attending secular universities) may feel uncomfortable holding on to their belief amid a community of unbelievers. Consequently, they soon discover that it is more comfortable accepting the nonbelief of their community. In such cases, faith is rejected for the sake of comfort and acceptance by their peers. This scenario is more likely if their conviction has little biblical foundational support. (This is why biblical knowledge and understanding are so necessary.)

Many who embrace a new or nonbelief system may do so simply because it's more comfortable or safer to do so. But, of course, the opposite is also true. Others may hold to their present beliefs, even when faced with truths that repudiate them. Why? Because by doing so, they can remain in their comfort zone. Deception is the desired choice when people value comfort above truth.

> Our inward desire and the comfort around us contribute to our succumbing to the deception before us.

The term *biblical conviction* refers to what happens when the Holy Spirit uses a truth from the Bible to convict (convince) someone that they need to change their beliefs, attitudes, and actions. Today, however, many are experiencing comfort conviction. They are convincing themselves of the need to abandon their old beliefs because they no longer provide comfort. A move to a new community, establishing a new relationship, or landing a new job, often brings the temptation to adopt the beliefs held by those within their newly acquired environment for the sake of one's treasured comfort.

Our inward desire and the comfort around us contribute to our succumbing to the deception before us. But, unfortunately, a lack of critical thinking also enhances the power of deceivers.

Lack of Critical Thinking

We are often gullible and too trusting of others. We believe most (if not everything) that we read on the internet and see on television, provided it comes from a source that tells us what we want to hear. A little critical thinking can go a long way in rendering deceivers and their deceptions powerless. (Critical thinking is simply gathering all the available facts about a subject, analyzing them, and then making a rational and logical judgment or decision about the matter.)

However, a lack of critical thinking can produce a bumper crop of false doctrines and erroneous beliefs. It can also help to explain the growing acceptance of self-identifying as the opposite sex. Accepting this narrative as valid means accepting what someone feels, desires, or believes over what we see with our eyes, and science declares with its data.

Feelings have become the new reality, the new trump card. It trumps facts, truth, and science. It shows up in religious circles, as well as social settings. Science tells us that no constructive surgery can biologically change a male into a female or vice versa. Our DNA is unchangeable. However, feelings and desires have replaced facts as the new benchmark. The problem is not that a person is of the wrong sex but the wrong mindset. Such a person is discontent with their gender.

Our gender is not determined by our beliefs or desires but by unchangeable truths, like DNA. However, if our desire for something is strong enough, no evidence, facts, or truths will convince us otherwise. Thus, deception becomes our delight and data our detriment.

Herd Mentality

Satan has more tools than a mechanic. Suppose the comfort zone or lack of critical thinking is not enough to mislead and misdirect us. In that case, Satan will tap into our followers' mindset. (There's a good reason Jesus called us sheep.) Unfortunately, most people are followers, not leaders. In the fantasy story of the Pied Piper, Hamelin, Germany, was infested with rats. In desperation, the mayor agreed to pay a man in pied clothing if he could rid the town of the infestation. This mysterious man used his magic pipe to lure the rats to a body of water where they drowned. However, the mayor reneged on his promised payment. In retaliation, the piper lured all the children away from town while the adults were in church. The children were never heard from again.

Sociologists tell us there is no need for a magical pipe. All it takes is a small minority to lead the majority down the wrong path and into the land of falsehoods. It's called *herd mentality.*

It is a powerful psychological force. It can shape and mold us, overriding our moral compass and common-sense thinking. It can cause us to do and say things out of character and unbecoming. But, besides making wrong choices and poor decisions, it can move us to make the right choices, but for the wrong reasons.

Even before I had heard the term *herd mentality*, I recognized it as a problem in group settings such as vacation Bible school and church camps. I didn't have to attend many to realize something wasn't right. Don't misunderstand; I think church camps and VBS are beautiful tools for sharing the gospel. I also don't have a problem giving an invitation (as long as the children are old enough to understand the gospel and someone thoroughly explains it).

However, we should use extreme caution in giving mass invitations. There is a legitimate concern that children will respond to the group invitation simply because their friend went forward or thought it's what the adults want. When we push them into praying or confessing Christ as their Savior, we cannot be good shepherds. We need to consider how children think and how their emotions work. Children may come to the altar not out of conviction but because of the mindset of the herd. Children who respond to an altar call while popping their gum, smiling, and giggling do not indicate a conviction of the Spirit. So, if we push them into praying and confessing Jesus as Lord, we may make them twice a child of hell because we have given them a false conversion.

When giving an altar call, use wisdom and spiritual discernment. Be aware of the dangers of herd mentality. Not

> If our primary concern is the child's salvation, and it should be, we will ask questions, discern faces, and tread lightly.

everyone who responds to an invitation is necessarily being drawn by God. If more than one responds, the power of the herd could be at work.

Therefore, we must be very discerning when dealing with impressionable children. I say this because I have been there. I know what it's like to have someone urging you into deciding for Christ instead of being saved by Christ. And there is a difference, a big difference. If our primary concern is the child's salvation, and it should be, we will ask questions, discern faces, and tread lightly.

Children who lack a basic understanding of the gospel--what it means to be lost, saved, or how Jesus' death and resurrection figure into the equation are highly unlikely (although nothing is impossible to God) to be drawn by the Holy Spirit. The Holy Spirit works in conjunction with the Holy Scriptures, not apart from them. He uses truth, biblical truth. So be on guard, for deception can occur amid our earnest desire to see children come to Christ. Don't let Satan use your love for kids to deceive you into watering down what it means to be saved from a conscious commitment to Christ to a simple decision for Christ.

Don't discount the cunningness of the master deceiver. Don't let Satan take something good (which he does regularly) and turn it into something terrible. An altar call, if done right, can save children, but one done wrong can deceive both children and adults.

So, adults, be on guard. Satan uses herd mentality on us just as effectively as on children. Are we not seeing it alive and well throughout society? Are we not currently witnessing an unprecedented upheaval in race relations, disregard for law and order, rejection of science in gender identification, and attacks upon our national heritage and constitutional form of government? Is Satan using herd mentality to deceive us into destroying our way of life?

The Nazi movement began with a small group that influenced the majority. They used bullhorns and rallies to brainwash the people. Today's herd influencers need only a social media account and a few loyal followers who will share their message. Then, combine a bias media promoting a dangerous message while barring opposing views, and you have the perfect storm for creating and stampeding a herd.

Unfortunately, when emotions trump facts and science, deception wins, Satan wins, and God's order for humanity is rejected and re-scripted.

Our decisions and understanding about life and community should be based on truth, not feelings. God's word and accurate scientific data are valid and should always hold sway over emotions and feelings. But, unfortunately, America's prevailing mindset and its laws and those of the world are increasingly being shaped by feelings and emotions, which the herd masters have stirred up.

Satan is the master of deception. But, thankfully, we don't have to succumb to him or grope blindly in the fog of delusion.

Because truth, when it is received, can part the fog that deludes us and liberate us from the hand that enslaves us, the hand of Satan.

Deliverance from Deception

Unfortunately, there are no areas immune to deception. We are not perfect; we are not God; therefore, we can be, have been, and will probably be deceived again. Thus, deception is a reality we must face, but it doesn't have to be a state in which we live. There is a pathway out of it, but it is narrow and often untraveled. It usually begins in the comfort zone, runs through the rough terrain of critical thinking and over the herd mentality mountains, and ends in the land of truth.

> Only those who acknowledge the existence of undiscovered truths are open to receiving them when they knock.

The first unpleasant truth we must face is that we don't have all the truth. Only those who acknowledge the existence of undiscovered truths are open to receiving them when they knock. Truth is the key to our deliverance from deception. If new truths (truths that we are unaware of) knock on our doors, we must receive them with all readiness of mind.

Are you willing? I hope so, for it is the only ticket out of a world of deception. However, avoiding deception and breaking free from it doesn't come easy. After breaking free, we must be forever on guard to continue in freedom. We must stay alert because our sinful nature is a sucker for manufactured spiritual paths, which provide no answers to the universal problem of sin.

Many embrace the idea that religion is the way to God. However, church membership or attendance can't save us. Religion, no matter how sincere, won't wash our sins away. So how can we know if what we believe is true? How can we know what is best for us, our families, and our church? How can we be sure of the path that leads to God and eternal life?

As we try to answer these questions, remember what matters most. It is not how strongly we believe, how long we have believed, or how comfortable we are with what we believe. What matters most is the evidence. The jury sits, listens, evaluates, and then decides based on the evidence during a trial. Therefore, if we want confidence in what we believe, we must do the same. Do you have the evidence you need for a confident belief in the Bible? Do you have truths to back up your beliefs and convictions? Can you explain what you believe and why you believe it?

A spiritual journey must be more than a stroll through the churchyard. It must be more like a jungle expedition searching for facts, pieces of evidence, and undiscovered truths that will give you the answers you need for the life you want. However, during this journey, you will be tempted to take shortcuts. Beware of the shortcuts.

Chapter 3:
The Shortcuts to Avoid

I discovered that shortcuts are not the way to go when searching for God. Yet, many people have and continue to try shortcuts; I know I did. Although I was not raised in a religious household, my parents did believe in God. But we were like so many who accepted the existence of God and that Jesus was God's Son. We even occasionally prayed. But our lives were guided, not by the Scriptures, but by moralistic principles.

But then, the truth of God's Word came knocking. It forced me to face an unpleasant truth about a universal problem. I had a sin problem that a spiritual shortcut couldn't fix. I discovered I was living under a cloud of deception while singing the songs of the gospel. I was lost spiritually but thought I was saved eternally.

How could I have been so deceived? It happened because I took a shortcut to God. But instead of God, I ended up with a cultural Christianity, which is both Christless and useless. My wrong turn occurred that night when my friend and her dad took my brother and me to the tent meeting, which I mentioned earlier. Although I didn't realize it as I took my first step toward

> The surprising thing about religion is that it inoculates you from God. We neither seek God nor are we open to God when we think we have God.

the front of the tent, I began my spiritual journey, but by the wrong road. However, many years later, I would realize that I had taken a shortcut that led me, not to God, but into religion.

The surprising thing about religion is that it inoculates you from God. We neither seek God nor are we open to God when we think we have God. Religion creates a false connection with God. Could many who claim to have abandoned God or left the Christian faith have only abandoned their faulty connection? Could they have left behind a religious mindset and system that they equated as a relationship with God?

The spiritual shortcut I took, left me lost and deluded. As a young boy, I was suddenly confronted with a universal problem of sin, the wrath of God, and the flames of hell, which were a lot to consider. It happened so quickly it was like a dream. To hook me up with God, a well-meaning evangelist and a good-hearted pastor, combined to make me a professor of faith without enabling me to become a possessor of God.

I don't remember the songs or the sermon that night, but I remember the invitation. It was well crafted. It was compelling. It was clear. It was straightforward. "Heaven or hell, which will it be? Turn or burn; it's your choice. If heaven, raise your hand. If you're serious, stand on your feet. Now come forward." So, we did. My brother and I both went to the front of the tent.

After we reached the front, they took us to a curtained-off section. We were quickly presented with an unfamiliar gospel (we were unchurched), encouraged to decide for Christ, asked to pray a specific prayer (known as the sinner's prayer), and then thoroughly assured, "You're now saved. You've asked

> Unfortunately, for me, nothing happened. I'm not talking about angels singing and fireworks exploding. I mean, nothing happened.

Christ into your heart, and He is faithful to come. Don't let anyone tell you otherwise. You're a child of God."

Unfortunately for me, nothing happened. I'm not talking about angels singing and fireworks exploding. I mean, nothing happened. Despite the efforts of a local pastor, I didn't have a desire to go to church, read my Bible, or share the gospel. There were no signs of spiritual fruit and no passion for spiritual things. The only thing I had from that night was the statement, "You're saved, and don't let anyone tell you otherwise." I didn't need God from that moment on because I supposedly had Him. My gospel (not Jesus') was all wrapped up in one thing, a decision. Understand me. It takes a decision. We can't become followers of anything or anyone without deciding to follow. But in Christianity, the decision is only one aspect of salvation.

Salvation is how God opens the gates of heaven for us. It puts us on the pathway to heaven and away from death and hell. A decision to follow Christ is a part of the process known as salvation, but it's not in any way meant to be the all-in-all of salvation. Unfortunately, I had unknowingly embraced hypocrisy. I left that tent meeting living a lie, but it would be several years before I would realize it.

Jesus warns about such shortcuts:

> Enter by the narrow gate. For the gate is wide
> and the way is easy that leads to destruction, and
> those who enter by it are many. 14 For the gate
> is narrow and the way is hard that leads to life,
> and those who find it are few. (Matthew 7:13-
> 14)

The narrow gate and the hard way will lead to true peace, inner fulfillment, and eternal life. But according to Jesus, there will be few who find it. Why? Because we are suckers for shortcuts, easy trails, and spiritual roads without tolls (commitment).

In the search for spiritual contentment, inner peace, and a sense of purpose, we must be on guard against the temptation of shortcuts. They promise spiritual fixes, guilt-relief without confession, and forgiveness without repentance, but they do not deliver. So, if you are offered peace with no spiritual substance, a sense of wholeness that's incomplete, a sense of spirituality void of power, and the promise of heaven without salvation, just say no. When we resist the Devil, he will flee from us and take his counterfeit salvation with him.

The all-inclusive, ever-accommodating, don't offend anyone philosophy promoted as the gospel is nothing more than a commercialized shortcut. Those who take it travel far from

> In a world of irresponsibility, we must take responsibility for every area of our lives, physical and spiritual.

God and into a world of religion and a lifetime of bondage. The unpleasant truth we must all face is we could be wrong—we could be living under a cloud of deception. We may have taken a shortcut amid all the spiritual fog in this world.

Spiritual Responsibility

In a world of irresponsibility, we must take responsibility for every area of our lives, physical and spiritual. The experts we look to can misinform, mislead, and make life miserable for us. They are human. They make mistakes. Even well-meaning doctors, nurses, ministers, and pastors are not perfect.

For instance, medical workers are experts in physical and mental health, but we must still take responsibility for our health. We cannot leave it totally to our physician or nursing staff. They could be incompetent. They could prescribe the wrong medication. Nurses and doctors can make mistakes.

When I was about 16 or 17 years old, I received a weekly allergy injection. On one particular day, the regular nurse was on vacation. The substitute nurse had worked for this doctor before, so I knew her. But as she was about to inject the serum, I noticed that the dosage was much larger than I'd ever received. Although she's the expert and I'm not, it's my arm and my life, so I spoke up. I said, "I see that my doctor has really upped the amount of serum." She then questioned me about what I meant. My response prompted her to recheck the prescribed dosage. She then thanked me several times for speaking up. She was about to inject me with one cc of a serum instead of one-tenth of a cc. Ten times, the prescribed amount could have sent me into anaphylaxis shock, possibly resulting in my death. We have to be responsible. We have to be observant. We have to take an active interest in our physical and spiritual health. Therefore, when someone offers us spiritual shortcuts or supposed new truths, search the Scriptures to see "What saith the Lord?"

Furthermore, hoping things will turn out okay is not a plan. It is not taking responsibility. Therefore, one must do more than hope and dream about going to heaven and living eternally in bliss.

Being an idealist is okay, but we must be willing to face reality. Don't fall for the bait used by con people. They offer cell revitalizing vitamins, miracle anti-aging creams, and special potions that can sustain sexual virility and physical longevity, but they can't deliver. Furthermore, eventually, reality comes knocking. Realists understand that no escape tunnels, back door exits, magic wardrobes, or mirrors can take us to a land without death.

The reality of death forces us to open our minds to the validity of spirituality. The certainty of death is why we need to evaluate our beliefs and their foundation. We need to know the truth, not someone's version of it. We need to have confidence that our belief is the right solution to our problem. Does it have the support of a trusted and proven source?

Although I had a belief system early on, it had little substance. Although I was confident I was on my way to heaven, my confidence was based on faulty premises and manufactured promises loosely tied to Scripture passages. Am

I the lone exception? I don't think so. Could it happen to others? Absolutely. Could it be true of you? You decide.

Could this be one reason many Christian teens are dropping out of church? Have they been duped into believing they are Christians, when in fact, they have embraced religiosity? In 2007 Lifeway Research surveyed more than 1,000 adults between the ages of 18-30 who had attended a Protestant church for at least one year during high school. According to the study, 70 percent of young adults ages 23-30 stopped attending church regularly for at least a year between ages 18-22. "[3]

Could this also be why, in my 30-plus years as a pastor, I have observed those whose beliefs cannot give them peace and security when faced with death? If we don't anchor our beliefs to a biblical foundation, the winds of life will blow them away when we need them the most, during the storms of life and in times of death.

Misinformation, missing information (spiritual ignorance), and eisegesis, the reading of one's ideas into a biblical text rather than the correct interpretation of the text, create a host of false and unsupported beliefs. Moreover, this ignorance leaves one's beliefs susceptible to the enemy's attacks and one's own internal doubts and fears.

Therefore, we must take responsibility for our spiritual growth and health. It is also why the Bible instructs believers to "But grow in the grace and knowledge of our Lord and Savior Jesus Christ" (2 Peter 3:18). This growth helps to provide the security and peace needed when death approaches. Furthermore, our children and grandchildren also need to grow

> Any shortcut that bypasses in-depth biblical knowledge, is a shortcut to a spiritual twilight zone where beliefs are many, but realities are few.

spiritually so their beliefs and convictions can stand firm when confronted by other religions or supposed contradictions by science. However, this growth doesn't just happen; it requires effort, learning, and time.

Any shortcut that bypasses in-depth biblical knowledge is a shortcut to a spiritual twilight zone where beliefs are many, but realities are few. Christian beliefs, not anchored to biblical truths, cannot survive in an ever increasingly pluralistic, atheistic, skeptical, post-Christian world. Therefore, I ask. Are your beliefs anchored to the solid rock of biblical truth? If not, they should be.

Unfortunately, it would be many years before I would discover that the shortcut I took provided me with false hope of heaven by false premises and incomplete truths.

When I returned home from that tent meeting, I was twice a child of hell. Sadly, I had falsely believed that I was safe spiritually. Several years later, I began attending a small church, but it would be another two years before realizing my deception. My shortcut to God took me down the road of illusion and into a land of counterfeits.

Just as pain medicine can mask our real problem, a false conversion can mask our actual need for God. A false conversion allows us to join a church, sing with the best of them, and sleep well at night. However, it doesn't transform us.

Unfortunately, counterfeit salvation is as common as gamblers at a horse race, except there are no winners. All the major religions offer some type of spiritual salvation. But are they simply providing false illusions? Is Christianity the only way, or is it just one of many to heaven, as often claimed? We must ask these questions along the way. And we must never settle for shortcuts to God.

Follow the Directions

Many signs that provide directions and essential information confront us when traveling on the highways. We trust them because of their source, the United States Transportation Department. The same is true for our spiritual journey. We need a source we can trust.

Thankfully, there is a source we can trust. There is a way to avoid deadly shortcuts. We need to look for signs showing how Christianity differs from other religions. We need something that can help us avoid those fatal shortcuts. The Bible provides the information necessary to avoid the dangerous shortcuts we don't need.

> Although we cannot comprehend the Bible without the Holy Spirit, we also cannot understand it without using our brains.

The Bible reveals that Christianity is based on faith, but not blind faith. On the contrary, it's based on a faith that makes logical sense within the framework of God's redeeming plan. But, don't misunderstand me; the Bible is not clear to those not connected to God, for they cannot understand the truths of God without the help of the Holy Spirit.

Without the Holy Spirit, the Bible, the Christian faith, and many other spiritual issues will not make sense.

> The natural person does not accept the things of
> the Spirit of God, for they are folly to him, and
> he is not able to understand them because they
> are spiritually discerned. (1 Corinthians 2:14)

Although we cannot comprehend the Bible without the Holy Spirit, we cannot understand it without using our brains. Becoming a Christian should not cause us to check our brains at the foot of the altar or the door of the church. So, I ask you to open your mind and carefully weigh the information provided in the upcoming chapters. Don't try taking shortcuts by bypassing certain sections.

Regardless of what you believe about Christianity or a particular branch of Christianity, make sure your belief and decisions are based on biblical knowledge. Beware of the dangers of spiritual shortcuts. And be sure to examine the truths of the Bible honestly and openly.

Shortcuts may play a significant role in why people claim Christ as Savior yet deny Him as Lord. It may be why some worship God on Sundays but forget Him on Mondays. Shortcut believers may claim to love God while harboring hatred and bitterness toward others. They say they believe the Word of God but pick the parts of the Bible they will and will not obey. Shortcuts create enormous problems. Taking spiritual shortcuts results in theological confusion. They bypass fundamental biblical teachings on such things as the depraved nature of humanity, the demands of God's holiness, the essentialness of faithfulness, the lordship of Jesus, and the reality of heaven and hell.

In contrast, the right path to heaven is paved with biblical knowledge. When we view the Bible with an open and honest mind, the Holy Spirit assists us in seeing the truths embedded in it, including the necessity of salvation and the means to it. I realize this position is often viewed as arrogant, narrow-minded, and exclusionary. Such a statement would be guilty of these accusations if it were not true, but it is true. Since it is true, it is not an arrogant conclusion but a truth that we should share for the good and benefit of others.

The allurement of shortcuts is why we must remain vigilant. Therefore, be on guard. Be alert. Be honest with yourself. If our faith is not based solely on God's Word, it has an unstable

> If our faith is not based solely on God's Word, it has an unstable foundation that will crumble when the storms of life and the blasts of skepticism come our way.

foundation that will crumble when the storms of life and the blasts of skepticism come our way.

There are no shortcuts to discovering the truth. We have to ask questions. We have to search the Scriptures. We cannot be satisfied with what others say about the Scriptures, regardless of whether they promote or denounce them. We must check them out for ourselves. Why? Well, the Bible is the key to discerning between a road that leads to heaven and one that leads to hell. The Bible gives us a clear and vivid picture of salvation. Although listening to others who share, teach, and preach from the Bible is good, we should confirm their words by the words of Scripture.

> The Bible gives us a clear and vivid picture of salvation.

We see why this is important from the biblical account of two men, Paul and Silas. Paul had been hostile to the Christian faith. He had done everything he could to stomp it out. But after being confronted by the resurrected Jesus, Paul obeyed Christ's command. He began preaching and teaching that Christ was the Son of God, the way to God, and the pathway to eternal life.

However, the people in the city of Berea were not content with just hearing his take on it. The Bereans searched the Old Testament to determine if he spoke the truth. They wanted biblical confirmation of what he had told them. They were not willing to take a shortcut to spiritual knowledge.

Now these Jews were more noble than those in
Thessalonica; they received the word with all
eagerness, examining the Scriptures daily to see
if these things were so. [12] Many of them
therefore believed, with not a few Greek women
of high standing as well as men." (Acts 17:11-
12)

After they consulted the Scriptures, the Bereans became
believers because they confirmed that Paul and Silas spoke the
truth about God, Jesus, and salvation. This kind of confirmation
is still needed. We need to examine and measure all spiritual
teachings by the Scriptures—the ultimate spiritual yardstick.
We need to be like Sergeant Joe Friday of the old television
series *Dragnet*, who said that *all we need are the facts, just the
facts.* In our case, we need spiritual truths found in the Bible.

According to many, the Bible is unnecessary for
spirituality. A Google search is sufficient for most.
Consequently, the air is full of unbiblical and unfounded
beliefs. Some common beliefs are "Just be sincere about what
you believe. That's what matters" "Christ died for everyone so
that everyone will be saved, regardless of what they believe or
how they live."

Many have bought into universalism, believing that all
religions are equal and will take everyone to the same place—
heaven, but through different avenues. Unfortunately, many
have accepted these and other beliefs as true. Sadly many are
mistakenly confident about their salvation. Mark Twain said,

"It ain't what you don't know that gets you into trouble. It's what you know for sure that just ain't so."

An increasing number of people are wrongly satisfied that there's nothing from which to be saved. According to Lifeway Research Center, "A majority of Americans (56%) say hell is a real place where some will be punished forever."[4]

These results mean 44% don't believe in the existence of hell. Unfortunately, many ministers and churches soft-sell the doctrine of hell or avoid it altogether. It is rarely, if ever, emphasized in most sermons by well-known television ministers. (Just tune them in, and you will see.)

The problem is that Satan has deceived many into believing they must embrace marketing techniques to the point of scrapping objectionable doctrines such as hell. When the guardians of the gospel—pastors and priests—sidestep important doctrinal truths such as hell, sin, and the need for salvation, Satan fills this vacuum with manufactured avenues to heaven.

Shortcuts that navigate around a belief in hell will soon, if not already, avoid a belief in the sinfulness of man, the wrath of God, and the judgment of God. It will eventually bypass the necessity of Christ's death to deal with our sin problem and the judgment facing us. Shortcuts may save us time, effort, and miles when traveling, but they can be a shortcut to hell in the spiritual realm.

Salvation cannot be based on or shaped by opinion polls or Madison Avenue marketing techniques. Only God can determine it, for only God has the authority to do so. He defines the when, what, why, and how of it. He decides the reason for it, the changes it produces, the benefits it provides, the pathway to it, and how to have the assurance of it.

Genuine assurance of salvation is vital, but it requires a clear understanding of the who, what, and how of salvation. We must know the who's who of salvation before we can grasp the certainty of it and have confidence in it. We must know who does the saving, who needs saving, and how it is accomplished. We can't obtain this kind of information through shortcuts. We can't find it under a rock, in a dream, or on the internet (apart from the Bible). It must be given to us, unveiled for us, and received by us. God has provided all we need in a book we call the Book of books—the Bible.

Therefore, we need a thorough understanding of what the Bible teaches about this specific, essential, life-changing, soul-saving issue. However, this book is not an all-inclusive study of the doctrine of salvation (Soteriology) or an in-depth understanding of the doctrine of heaven (Ouranology). However, it offers insights for the non-scholarly person who desires a sure salvation by a wonderful Savior who provides eternal life in a glorious place called heaven.

Heaven is too important and eternity is too long to be seduced by the lure of shortcuts that lead to a counterfeit heaven that is no heaven at all. So, we must resist the temptation of shortcuts and guard against embracing counterfeit salvations.

Chapter 4:
The Counterfeit Salvation

Counterfeit money may look like the real thing, but it's not. It's a worthless imitation. The same is true of a counterfeit salvation. It may give us a sense of peace, but its eternal value is worthless. It doesn't appease the anger of God or open the doors of heaven. Worst of all, many unknowingly promote it as the real thing. I know because I once was a victim of it. Although it doesn't save and transform, it can provide a sense of spirituality and security while offering no spiritual power.

Counterfeit conversions are a real and present problem in the world of Christianity. Many of the Pharisees and Sadducees were in this category. They had a false sense of spiritual security. After all, they were the children of Abraham. They were God's chosen people. They had the law of Moses and the promises of God. They were sure they were right with God, even though they were far from God. The same can be true today. If we say the right words, believe the right things, and recite the proper prayer, we are assured by others and convinced

> Decisions to receive (accept) Christ have always played a role in salvation. However, something changed in the last century; a decision for Christ became the "all in all" of salvation instead of a part of the process.

in our hearts that we are saved, safe, and secure. But are we? Unfortunately, a life without God is bad enough, but it becomes worse when living under the delusion of having God.

When the lifestyles of the "born-agains" match those of the "sin-and-be-happy" crowd, the problem of false conversions and counterfeit Christians is evident. But is there more to it than mistaken people falling for false conversions and embracing counterfeit salvations? Is there a counterfeit conspiracy at work? Are the demons of hell working with the deceived to promote and produce fake conversions?

After all, Satan is a master deceiver and the father of lies. He relentlessly takes the good and corrupts it. Decisions to receive (accept) Christ has always played a role in salvation. However, something changed in the last century; a decision for Christ became the "all in all" of salvation instead of a part of the process. It was elevated to mean what it was never meant to convey.

Furthermore, if a simple decision for Christ settles the issue of salvation, there would be no need for biblical confirmation of one's salvation. Yet, the Bible is full of telltale signs and bold declarations of how salvation changes us, transforms us, and assures us that we are saved, redeemed, and delivered from the bondage of Satan and the power of sin.

The Bible boldly emphasizes the radical change that salvation brings. Consequently, we need to unearth a seemingly hidden truth buried in religious jargon. The Bible never directs us to look back at the moment in time or a specific event or

> The Bible never directs us to look back at a moment in time or a specific event or decision as evidence of our salvation. Instead, it focuses on the life of Christ lived out by the believer.

decision as evidence of our salvation. Instead, it focuses on the life of Christ lived out by the believer. It focuses on the present, not the past. It emphasizes a changed life, not a prayer prayed or a decision made.

A ritual is not the way to God. It didn't work in the Old Testament, and it doesn't work in the New Testament. Praying a prayer, confessing one's sins, and deciding for Christ makes for an easy three-step plan to connect with God. However, if the convicting power of the Holy Spirit is absent, so will be the saving power of God. Many counterfeit conversions occur because people choose Christ instead of responding to Christ. Salvation is not something you can purchase online or pick up at the supermarket. We can choose to look to Christ and cry out to Him, but in the end, salvation occurs when we surrender to the call of Christ.

Many factors can send us to our knees and pull a prayer out of our mouths. For instance, when our backs are against the wall, and all hope is fading, do we not pull the emergency cord of prayer.

Furthermore, the power of peer pressure is real. Adults and children both know what it's like to succumb to it. I fear that many people have prayed the sinners' prayer, not to please God, but to please their spouse, parents, or girl or boy, they are crazy about in school or church. However, the process of salvation begins when we have a sense of our sinfulness. Then we must recognize Christ and His saving work as the solution to it.

Unfortunately, we have embraced a religious solution to a present personal problem if we fail to do this. Thus, we are still in our sin but ignorant of it. It is conviction, not convenience, that is essential to salvation. The Holy Spirit plays a crucial role in our salvation. He must make our sins and the Savior real to us; He must convince (convict) us we are lost; He must provide the faith we need.

We must embrace this inescapable truth about salvation; it is the work of the Holy Spirit. Although its benefits are many, the primary purpose of salvation is to solve our sin problem, not our present predicament.

How could a counterfeit conversion be mistaken for the real deal? The answer is, easily, just redefine what it means to be a Christian and what a conversion involves. When we define it as a prayer prayed and a decision made, it's all about two deeds performed. If Christianity is just wearing a Christian label after saying a prescriptive prayer, it doesn't matter how we live. But if it's about committing our lives to Christ and making Him Lord and Savior, *and it is*, then it will produce a radical change.

I've heard it said that we shouldn't doubt our salvation. I believe we should and shouldn't. We shouldn't have doubts if Christ is real enough and the evidence is strong enough. But there should be doubts if there are reasons for doubting it. However, no Christian should live with doubts about their salvation. Thankfully, answers to critical questions can give us an unshakable confidence in our eternal salvation.

Is your salvation established on the proper foundation? Is it producing biblical results? Does it provide evidence that you have been transformed into a new creature in Christ? Do you have a desire for spiritual things? Are you bearing spiritual fruit? Do you hunger for righteousness? Is the old you fading and the new you forming? If not, then it should be doubted. If it can't stand before the light of the gospel, we should relegate it to the trash heap of religiosity, or better yet, trade it in for the real thing.

Satan works hard to get us to disregard any red flags that point to counterfeit salvation. For example, suppose Satan tricks us into focusing on a former emotional moment or a memorable event that we construe as evidence of our salvation. If so, he will keep us from noticing the red flags that God has embedded throughout the Bible. Satan may even use the peace and good emotions we experience after a good cry at the altar as evidence of our salvation.

But of course, internal peace is not always a sign of God's presence nor His approval. Satan uses anything and everything possible to mislead and confuse us. For instance, an emotional release, which may come from a good cry, can provide that sense of peace, but it has nothing to do with God's saving grace. It's the kind that occurs when we've struggled about committing an act the Scripture forbids and calls sin. However, after pushing ahead with it, we experience an emotional relief because the tension of the indecision is over. We view this absence of tension as God's peace when it is Satan's deception.

The story of Jonah is a good example. First, he struggled with obeying God's command to preach repentance to the Ninevites. Then, after deciding to disobey God, he bought a ticket and hopped on a ship, heading opposite of God's will. Following this, he experienced an emotional peace that allowed him to sleep soundly in the bottom of the ship while a storm was raging all around him (see Jonah 1:1-5). Unfortunately, a false peace may allow us to sleep soundly, but it will not protect us from the anger and judgment of God.

> Nowhere in the Bible do we see the actions or processes leading up to salvation or accompanying one's conversion as confirmation or assurance of one's conversion.

Don't let Satan push a counterfeit salvation on you by way of a phony conversion, and it can happen. I have not only experienced it but have known others who were victims of it. I've come across far too many people whose attitudes and actions were anything but Christ-like and God-honoring, yet they were sure of their salvation. Why are they sure? They base their confidence on a prayer prayed or a seemingly spiritual experience. I know people who point to the fact that they've been slain in the spirit, levitated off their couch, propelled to shout and run around the church, etc., as proof of their salvation.

Nowhere in the Bible do we see the actions or processes leading up to salvation or accompanying one's conversion as confirmation or assurance of one's conversion. Emotional experiences or supposed miraculous happenings are not reliable markers for true salvation. Now, I'm not saying emotional salvation experiences are not real; they can be. But they are not meant to provide us with the assurance of our salvation.

Counterfeit experiences can accompany fake conversions. Such experiences may even produce limited changes in one's lifestyles and behavior, but they fall short of what is produced by authentic conversions. Take note; Satan is the master imitator. He has always imitated the power of God to a limited degree. Counterfeit evidence of salvation is similar to the magic of Pharaoh's magicians. They duplicated the first two plagues put on Egypt by God, turning water into blood and bringing forth frogs. However, they could not repeat the rest of the plagues (see Exodus 8:18).

The problem with a counterfeit salvation is it never produces long-lasting, significant change because it doesn't transform a person. It is salvation without regeneration, which is one of Satan's greatest deceptions. Remember what Jesus said, "for he is a liar and the father of lies" (John 8:44).

The most effective means of preventing people from seeking God or receiving God's salvation is to convince them they don't need it or already have it. The following are just a couple of red flags for counterfeit conversions.

No Spiritual Appetite

The indwelling of the Holy Spirit should create a hunger for the things of God.

> Like newborn infants, long for the pure spiritual
> milk, that by it you may grow up to salvation—
> [3]if indeed you have tasted that the Lord is good.
> (1 Peter 2:2-3)

In the above passage, the apostle Peter encourages his readers, who he assumed were Christians, to desire spiritual food just like newborns desire milk. But he adds, "if indeed you have tasted that the Lord is good."

Suppose we have indeed tasted that the Lord is good, meaning that we have experienced His wonderful salvation. In that case, we should desire the pure spiritual milk—His Word. Counterfeit salvation will produce no spiritual appetite. However, the person who experiences a fake conversion will find that the Bible is still a closed book. The church has little appeal, and prayer is a burden rather than a pleasure.

No Spiritual Power

One of the most heartbreaking scenes is that of a person who wants to live right but doesn't have the power to do so. For instance, non-Christians reared by godly parents will desire to live according to their upbringing. Still, the spiritual strength to do so is absent. Unfortunately, a compounding factor is a mistaken belief they are Christians. Such a person understands the need to live righteously and holy for God. Still, without the power to do so, they experience guilt and despair. This lack of power can eventually lead to a distorted view of Christianity. In the end, a person may come to accept sin as a part of the

Christian life. Or, they find themselves mired in a pond of despair, even to the point of becoming suicidal because they feel hopelessly trapped in sin's bondage.

When sinful habits and desires are too powerful to resist or overcome, we must re-examine our conversion. The problem may not be that the sin is too powerful, but the Spirit is not present. Why would I say this? Because the power to live the Christian life is available to every Christian.

> But he said to me, "My grace is sufficient for you, for my power is made perfect in weakness." Therefore I will boast all the more gladly of my weaknesses, so that the power of Christ may rest upon me. 10 For the sake of Christ, then, I am content with weaknesses, insults, hardships, persecutions, and calamities. For when I am weak, then I am strong. (2 Corinthians 12:9-10)

The promise of His presence, His power, and His provisions are available to those who have the real thing. Do you have it? Do you have the Christ of the Bible? Does the Holy Spirit dwell within you? If so, surrender fully to Him. If not, heed the warnings and receive Jesus Christ as Lord and Savior.

After realizing I was under the spell of a false conversion, I came to know Christ as my Lord and Savior. The convicting work of the Holy Spirit, combined with various telltale signs, helped me realize that as a young boy, I had embraced religion, but not Christ.

One of the purposes of this book is to help readers identify various evidence concerning one's salvation and some telltale signs of an absence of salvation. Knowing where we stand spiritually is of the utmost importance because we cannot live the Christian life without the Spirit of Christ living within us.

This need for spiritual power is why we must ask probing questions along our journey. Is my spiritual power lacking? Do I have little or no spiritual appetite for the things of God? Do I lack evidence of a new heart, new spirit, and new life?

Heaven is real, and eternity is long; therefore, we cannot afford to ignore the warning signs that God places along our journey. God wants us saved, sure, and safe.

Heed the Warning

The *Titanic* is one of the most publicized and tragic shipwrecks in maritime history. The loss of life was heart-wrenching, and sadly, completely avoidable. The captain ignored and rejected several warnings from other ships. They warned him to slow down, don't travel at night, and take the longer, more southern route. But he was confident that his ship was unsinkable, so he went full steam ahead into an iceberg field. He refused to listen, and it cost him and others dearly.

God uses His Word, His Spirit, and His disciples to warn us. There is no need for us to sail full steam into the cold, dark, chilly waters of death, thinking (mistakenly) we are spiritually okay. God doesn't want us to leave this world with a false sense of confidence. He doesn't want us to think that the *Old Ship of*

> If we have a good grasp of what God says about salvation, we can know that we have eternal life, enjoy it more fully, and share it more faithfully.

Zion will carry us home, only to discover we got on the wrong ship—a counterfeit *ship of Zion.*

God has the only say about how salvation occurs, and He says Jesus is the only way. Therefore, God's Word, not our beliefs, our feelings, or the teachings of others, should provide us with the assurance of our salvation. If we have a good grasp of what God says about salvation, we can know that we have eternal life, enjoy it more fully, and share it more faithfully.

We need confidence in our salvation. We can have confidence. We can know that we are on the right road, headed in the right direction, and have the right salvation. We can know that the salvation that Christ provides is the one that we have. But it requires self-examination along the way. The philosopher Socrates said that *the unexamined life is not worth living.* For salvation, the unexamined life may be an unconverted one.

However, humility is necessary for us to embrace self-examination. But such an examination is worth it. We need an unshakable, unbreakable, and unchanging confidence in our salvation. And, of course, this kind of confidence comes only from the Word of God.

Chapter 5:
The Self-Examination

I've been there. We've all been there. Oh, the beauty, the joy, and the wonder of it all. When it happens, we want it to last forever. But then, we wake up. Dreams can be so real.

The joys of salvation and the beauty of heaven are real, but if we are not saved, they might as well be a dream. Only the saved can have the peace of God, the power of God, and

> Only the saved can have the peace of God, the power of God, and the promises of God as resources for living a life that honors God.

the promises of God as resources for living a life that honors God.

Therefore, we need to ask, could we be mistaken? Could we be wrong about our salvation? Could well-meaning friends, pastors, and family members have unintentionally misled us spiritually? The answer is YES! YES! They could have been wrong, and we could have mistaken a dream for reality and a false conversion for a real one. It happened to me, and it has happened to others.

The church community where I grew up was shocked when a well-respected local pastor confessed to his congregation that he had recently received Christ as Lord and Savior. He said, for many years, he was under the false impression that he was saved. He then resigned from his pastorate, concluding he could not have been called to the ministry when, in fact, he wasn't a Christian at the time of his calling.

He received criticism from many Christians and local pastors. I often heard statements like: *How could he not know? That's the silliest thing I've ever heard.* But I understand how it could happen, for I've been there. Good people make mistakes. Good people who receive terrible advice make significant mistakes, including equating an emotional experience or saying a prescriptive prayer with a genuine conversion.

Several years ago, a popular hiking magazine gave directions on how to come down from Britain's highest mountain safely during times of fog and mist. However, it provided wrong tips due to a sentence that was left out. If mountain climbers had followed the advice, it would have sent them over a 1,000 ft. cliff.

Fortunately, a climber noticed the mistake and got the word out. As a result, the magazine corrected its error in the following issue.

The wrong information about God's wonderful salvation can cause devastating consequences. Therefore, I want to get the word out. I want to warn those whom Satan and sin are blinding with their spiritual fog. For I, like many others, have in the past embraced a counterfeit salvation promoted by well-intentioned believers and ministers.

The magazine people made an honest, although potentially deadly, mistake. Unlike the enemy of our souls (who is intentional), believers and ministers make sincere mistakes.

> By the time I realized that I was not truly converted, I was a church member, sung in the choir, and was an assistant Sunday school superintendent.

However, Satan seeks to deceive and destroy us. He will take the Word of God and twist it to accomplish his will in our lives. He has taken the idea of deciding for Christ, which is a part of the salvation process, and made it the end. He has made a decision to receive Christ, more important than one to follow Christ. He has elevated a moment at an altar over that of a lifetime commitment.

Satan tried his deception on Jesus. His three wilderness temptations (See Matthew 4) were attempts at using passages from God's Word to trick Jesus into violating God's will. He continues to use this technique on believers and churches, but with much more success. I believe Satan did this to me those many years ago when he used others to pressure me into a false profession, resulting in a counterfeit conversion.

I know it's possible to redefine what it means to be saved, thus making it a non-redeeming type of salvation, which is no salvation at all.

I attended church for approximately two years before realizing my conversion was counterfeit. By the time I realized it, I was a church member, sung in the choir, and was the assistant Sunday school superintendent. I'm thankful God didn't give up on me, and the Holy Spirit continued to work on me. He convinced (convicted) me to reexamine my salvation.

The need for a reexamination is what the apostle Paul encouraged the Corinthians to do in their church.

> Examine yourselves, to see whether you are in the faith. Test yourselves. Or do you not realize this about yourselves, that Jesus Christ is in you?—unless indeed you fail to meet the test."
> (2 Corinthians 13:5)

After receiving Christ as Lord, I looked back with confusion at the events that led to my false profession. I had said all the right words and believed all the right things, so what was missing. The answer was—God. Salvation can make sense logically (fire insurance against the possibility of hell is logical), but it takes more than logic. It takes the convicting power of God. We must know the gravity of our sins, the fierceness of God's wrath, and the horribleness of hell before we can appreciate the wonder of His love.

I sought my salvation by logic, but God says it must come by His Spirit. Several years after my genuine conversion, while reading the Gospel of John, I experienced one of those *Ah-Ha* moments. It occurred when I read John 6:44. "No one can come to me unless the Father who sent me draws him. And I will raise him up on the last day."

> Unfortunately, our high capacity for self-deception allows Satan to dupe us easier than we can imagine.

It was then that I realized why I ended up with a false conversion experience. We can't secure a safe place in heaven according to our terms or by the rituals of men and women, but only by being drawn to Christ by His Spirit can we be saved. I do not believe a commitment to Christ without an awareness of our sinful condition will ever create a sustaining appreciation for the love of God and the work of Christ. We must realize our lost state before we willingly give control to Jesus, making Him Lord and Savior.

No wonder counterfeit conversions are so attractive. They offer, falsely, of course, fire insurance without commitment to Christ or His Word.

I'm sure many, like myself and the local pastor I shared about, have experienced counterfeit conversions. Unfortunately, our high capacity for self-deception allows Satan to dupe us easier than we can imagine. Consequently, bogus conversions have been a problem since the days of Jesus.

The first to fit this category was Judas Iscariot. He talked the talk. He looked forward to the benefits. But he was a follower in appearance only. Instead of being the center of his life, Jesus was simply a means to get what Judas wanted in life.

In the end, he gave up all pretense when something with more promise and quicker rewards came along. Thirty pieces of silver *in hand* were better than a kingdom *in the bush.* He betrayed someone he was associated with, not someone he

Sometimes the unconverted follower is a sincere seeker, someone searching for God.

viewed as the King of kings or as a brother he loved. In the end, the Bible tells us precisely who Judas was. He was not a believer. He was not a convert. What was he? He was a surface follower, an interested party, an opportunist. But most of all, he was the son of destruction, according to Jesus (see John 17:12).

Sometimes the unconverted follower is a sincere seeker, someone searching for God. They seek to honor God. They take part in the worship and the work of God, much like the pastor I shared about earlier. Unfortunately, John Wesley, the founder of the Methodist movement, was also the victim of a false conversion.

John was ordained as a member of the clergy in the church of England in 1728. In 1735, he was invited to serve as the pastor of the new colony of Georgia. During his journey, a massive storm engulfed the ship. His experience on the trip set in motion a self-examination of his relationship with God. According to John Telford, who authored "The Life of John Wesley:"

> Mr. Wesley being ashamed of his unwillingness to die, asked himself; 'How is it thou hast no faith.' The good impression already made on his mind by the humility and devotion of the Moravians was increased by their fearlessness in the tempest. He found that they were delivered from the spirit of fear, as well as from pride, anger, ... as they were singing a psalm the sea broke over the vessel split the main sail in piece and poured in between the decks as if the great

deep had already swallowed them up. The Germans calmly sang on. Even the women and children were not afraid to die. Their spirit made the deeper impression on Wesley because the English passengers were trembling and screaming with terror.

Mr. Telford later adds:

On the 5th of February, 1736, the Simmonds sailed into the Savannah river. Next morning, at eight, the emigrants set foot on American soil. Wesley and his friends knelt down with the Governor to thank God for their safety amid all the perils of the sea. Mr. Oglethorpe then took boat for Savannah, leaving the emigrants to assemble on shore and await his return. Next day he was with them again. Mr. Spangenberg, a Moravian minister from Savannah, came with him. Wesley sought his advice about his own work. Spangenberg asked him a few questions. His first inquiry, "Does the Spirit of God bear witness with your spirit that you are a child of God" surprised Wesley so that he did not know what to answer. The German observing this, asked, "Do you know Jesus Christ" He paused, and said, "I know He is the Saviour of the world." "True," was the reply; "but do you know He has saved you." Wesley answered, "I hope

He has died to save me." Spangenberg only added, "Do you know yourself?" Wesley replied, "I do." "But I fear they were vain words," is his comment.[5]

On May 24th, 1738, according to Mr. Wesley's diary, he went *unwillingly* to a Society in Aldersgate Street where someone was reading Luther's preface to the Epistle to the Romans. Mr. Wesley then writes in his diary,

> About a quarter before nine, while he was describing the change which God works in the heart through faith in Christ, I felt my heart strangely warmed. I felt I did trust in Christ, Christ alone, for salvation; and an assurance was given me, that He had taken away my sins, even mine, and saved me from the law of sin and death.[6]

I can't tell you the date I was saved, as did John Wesley (I didn't keep a diary.). But I remember vividly the night God showed me that I was wrong about my salvation and was then genuinely saved. I finally came to grips with my false conversion following a revival service. The convicting power of the Holy Spirit was on me when I kneeled beside my bed, poured out my heart to God, trusted in Jesus, and committed my

> We can be wrong; we can be mistaken. All of us are susceptible to misinformation, misguided people, misinterpretations, and misunderstandings.

life to Him. I suddenly was sure. The Spirit of God bore witness with my spirit that I was a child of God.

So beware, it can happen to the best of us. It can happen to the religious and non-religious. We can be wrong; we can be mistaken. All of us are susceptible to misinformation, misguided people, misinterpretations, and misunderstandings. We must acknowledge these possibilities. We must recognize the spiritual fog in our nation, world, churches, hearts, and minds. Therefore, we must be open to self-examination and reexamination. We must be open to truth, even those which may contradict our cherished beliefs and established way of life.

John Wesley, myself, and others have thought we were on the right road and headed in the right direction, yet we were wrong. Thankfully, we were wise enough to listen to others. We were honest enough to admit we could be wrong. We were smart enough to be open to the moving of the Holy Spirit. And most of all, we were willing to lay aside our pride and humbly accept the truth of our lostness and that our only solution was Christ and His work on the cross.

Whether we recognize it, the fog is there. It clouds our view of Christ. It blinds us to our lost condition. It may allow us to see the need for spirituality but hide the very One who is the key to it. But no matter how thick the fog is, truth has the power to penetrate it. When truth knocks, receive it, act on it, embrace it, and it will change your life. To do otherwise is to continue down the road of destruction. To do otherwise is to continue to live a lie. To do otherwise is to embrace a counterfeit conversion and salvation that provides a false comfort now but no hope later.

Chapter 6:
The Right Path

Benjamin Franklin realized that the newly formed constitution gave the appearance of permanency, so he writes, *but in this world nothing can be said to be certain, except death and taxes.* But is this true? Can we not also be sure of other things in life? Yes, we can. Although death is inevitable, life is also certainly too short. Eternity is undoubtedly long. And our eternal future is too important for us to be uncertain about it.

> We don't need just any road; we need the right path that will take us to our desired destination—heaven.

In my journey, I discovered many religions and many versions of Christianity that offer heaven or some facsimile thereof as our eternal retirement option, but most provide vague and uncertain means to get there. We don't need just any road; we need the right one to take us to our desired destination—heaven.

So, the search for truth in the realm of spirituality must be our top priority. But where can we find this kind of truth? Where should we look? Which yellow brick road is the right one? Many have looked to the deep thinkers, the philosophers throughout the centuries. Others have taken a more religious approach and have sought the theologians and spiritual leaders. In their search for truth, today's generation often goes to the holy grail of information—Google. The world's mindset is that every opinion is trustworthy, and everybody who gives an opinion is an expert. In our informational age, we have many choices, sources, and much misinformation, all of which Satan disguises as truth.

Surf the internet, or go to your local library and check out the religious magazines or bookstalls containing religious books. You will find that such sources are no respecter of nationalities, geographical locations, religious backgrounds, or language types. You also will discover them hard-selling their beliefs on how to get to heaven or their version of a heaven-like eternal resting place. With so much to choose from, is there a reliable source? Is there a sure and right road to travel?

The Bible

Earlier, I said that I believe the Bible was the place to go. I think it is the Rosetta stone of spirituality? But why it, above the other religious writings? The answer lies with an honest look at the Bible. Despite claims to the contrary, misinterpretations galore, and abusive uses, the Bible, with its long history of weathering attacks by entrenched communist rulers, atheist groups, and higher critical scholars, still stands tall among the religious literature of our world. But is it trustworthy? Can it stand the close examination of its critics as

> The Bible gives us the hope of eternal life and the basis for this hope.

to its accuracy, consistency, and relevancy? It not only can but has throughout the centuries.

Our modern age consistently provides discoveries by present-day archaeologists that support the accuracy and reliability of the Bible. The many archaeological findings that have verified cities and people of the Bible give the Bible much credence. However, the argument that if a city or person in the Bible doesn't have archaeological confirmation, then that person or city didn't exist holds no validity. Archaeology can provide evidence that something existed. However, it can't give proof of non-existence.

Although the Bible has been misused by some and opposed by many, its power to impact lives is undeniable. It is a book of truth. It provides us with a record of the good, the bad, and the ugly. In it, we see men and women who obeyed God, rejected God, failed God, misunderstood God, and were used by God. Furthermore, it reveals the power of God, the manifestation of God, the Son of God, and the salvation of humanity. The Bible gives us the hope of eternal life and the basis for this hope. It enables us to see the impossible become a reality and thus provides us with the hope of the impossible. It gives us strength when living and hope and comfort when dying.

According to Robert J. Morgan, it gave hope and comfort to President Andrew Jackson in his last moments. Mr. Morgan writes in his book *Near to the Heart of God* that after the president's conversion to Christianity, he developed a love for hymns. In June 1845, he was weak and near death. His daughter-in-law, Sarah Jackson, sat through the night with him. During the night, she noticed his lips moving. After bending near to the president, she heard the words, *"When through the deep waters I call thee to go ... "* Shortly afterward, Jackson died on June 8, 1845. The hymn that President Jackson was quoting was *How Firm a Foundation.*

> How firm a foundation, ye saints of the Lord,
> Is laid for your faith in His excellent Word!
> What more can He say than to you He hath said,
> You, who unto Jesus for refuge have fled?

> In every condition, in sickness, in health;
> In poverty's vale, or abounding in wealth;
> At home or abroad, on the land, or the sea,
> As thy days may demand, as thy days may demand,
> As thy days may demand, shall thy strength ever be.

> When through the deep waters I call thee to go,
> The rivers of woe shall not overflow;
> For I will be with thee, thy troubles to bless,
> And sanctify to thee thy deepest distress.

The soul that on Jesus has leaned for repose,
I will not, I will not desert to its foes;
That soul, though all hell should endeavor to shake,
I'll never, no never, no never forsake.[7]

Our faith's foundation is His excellent Word. The Bible provides us with a firm foundation, both in life and death. Those who deny it do so because they refuse to see it or are blinded by Satan, who hates it. The Bible is accurate, and it is powerful. The Bible says this about itself:

> For the word of God is living and active, sharper than any two-edged sword, piercing to the division of soul and of spirit, of joints and of marrow, and discerning the thoughts and intentions of the heart. 13 And no creature is hidden from his sight, but all are naked and exposed to the eyes of him to whom we must give account. (Hebrews 4:12–13)

Those who deny it likely do so because of intent, not content. The late apologist Ravi Zacharias once said, "Intent will always precede content." If one examines the Bible with an open mind and an honest desire to know its contents, they will recognize it is unique. They will discover that although men penned it, it is a book from God. But suppose one intends to prove it unreliable and full of errors regardless of the facts before them. In that case, they will see errors and contradictions

> Just as a compass used in math must have its center point to work out from, so does the search for eternal truth. The Bible is that point, for it has miraculously survived the fires of persecution and the storms of controversies throughout centuries of criticisms.

even where none are. Those with hostile intent will reject any evidence that contradicts their *apriori* (supposedly self-evident beliefs). Sadly, such people are unreachable because they are unteachable.

Unfortunately, many employ logical fallacies as an excuse for closing their minds to disliked and uncomfortable truths in the Bible. Others, such as Communist nations and dictatorships, simply ban it out of fear. They forbid its possession and arrest those who preach its contents. Their fear and hatred toward it reveal the power in it. They know it's not just another book. It is the Book of books. It is the Word of God, which is backed by the power of God. Those who fear it knows the power it contains and the changes it can bring. They know that it can set the captives free from oppression and abuse.

Despite its political incorrectness, the Bible is the place to go for God's sure salvation. Just as a compass used in math must have its center point to work out from, so does the search for eternal truth. The Bible is such a point, for it has miraculously survived the fires of persecution and the storms of controversies throughout centuries of criticisms. In it, we have God revealing Himself, His plan, and our eternal destination. It provides the knowledge we need for the eternal truths we desire. Any so-called avenues to eternal life that are not biblically paved are simply dead-end streets. These so-called pathways will one day fade, fail, and fall apart over time, as do all man-made objects. In the end, humanly paved avenues will lead all who travel them to a shocking and disastrous final non-resting place.

For a sure and solid salvation, you need to look no further. The Bible provides the guidelines, framework, foundation, and assurance of salvation. We need nothing else. The Bible suffices to enlighten us, sustain us, and equip us for this life and beyond. It provides the pathway to eternal life, which is called salvation.

In salvation, the Bible is all we need. We don't need Congress to approve it, the philosophers to debate it, or Facebook to like it. The only thing we need is to embrace the truth of God's Word and the desires of God's heart. God has revealed Himself and His plan in the Bible because of His love. He desires that we spend eternity with Him. His means for accomplishing it is called salvation, which His Son provided.

The best part about salvation is that we don't have to be confused, uncertain, or misled about it. The apostle John writes, "I write these things to you who believe in the name of the Son of God, that you may know that you have eternal life" (1 John 5:13).

We can know that we are saved, and eternal life is ours. But for us to know for sure, we must embrace more than theological concepts. We need truths that can anchor us in a world of ever-changing beliefs and uncertainties, and we find them in the Bible. If we have a firm grip on the biblical teachings of salvation, we can have unshakable confidence in our salvation. Consequently, we can experience the abundant life Jesus refers to in John 10:10, "... I came that they may have life and have it abundantly."

> Jesus's resurrection provided the victory over death. However, if we want to have victory over our fear of death, we must apply His victory to our fears.

Abundant Life

Those who travel the right path to salvation can experience the pure joy of the abundant life. We live in a life-draining, joy-sucking, dream-shattering, and heart-breaking world, so the idea of an abundant life is appealing and stimulating, but most of all, impossible. But impossible, it is not. The abundant life is not only possible; it can be a reality, but only after the fear of death is removed from life's itinerary.

Before the abundant life can be ours, death must lose its sting. Death must be defeated. The good news is that Jesus has transformed death into a doorway to heaven. When God saves us, He does away with any need to fear death. The Bible proclaims:

> Death is swallowed up in victory. [55] O death, where is your victory? O death, where is your sting? [56]The sting of death is sin, and the power of sin is the law. [57]But thanks be to God, who gives us the victory through our Lord Jesus Christ. (1 Corinthians 15:54-57)

Jesus's resurrection provided victory over death. However, if we want to have victory over our fear of death, we must apply His victory to our fears. Our faith in Christ and His Word gives us the confidence we need to defeat the fear we dread. But this kind of confidence doesn't just happen. It can't be a hand-me-down, second-hand kind of confidence. It can't be given by relatives, Sunday school teachers, or faithful pastors.

Such confidence must be built with solid materials and anchored to the solid rock of truth. It must withstand the cold, bitter winds of a disease-riddled body and the devastating death of a loved one. It must be able to endure a heartbreaking divorce, the cold logic of non-believers, and the nightmarish

Anyone who accepts Jesus as Lord and Savior has eternal life, but this doesn't mean they have the assurance of it and confidence in it.

conditions and sufferings that fill our world. It has to stand firm even when the fiery darts of doubt and disbelief are directed at us by the demons of hell and the Devil himself.

Anyone who accepts Jesus as Lord and Savior has eternal life, but this doesn't mean they have the assurance of it and confidence in it. Therefore, we need a steadfast hope that comes not from within but from above. Our hope must be in Christ alone, as conveyed by the Word of God.

Unfortunately, many are confident, but for the wrong reasons. We must build our confidence with material that will never fade, fail, or falter. Many are confident in a foundation comprising wood, hay, and stubble (see 1 Corinthians 3:12). This kind of confidence relies on the speculations of men, the wisdom of philosophers, the accepted ideas of the masses, and the emotions of the moment. It has no depth, no sustaining power, and no biblical basis. It will eventually be uprooted by conflicting emotions, new philosophies, or the fickleness of the masses.

We saw earlier how the apostle John stressed the need for confidence in one's eternal state in 1 John 5:13. The God who created us understands our need for certainty, but do we? For us

---

Beauty may be in the eye of the beholder, but salvation is not. God's Word, not human opinions or speculations, provides the knowledge we need for the salvation we claim and the confidence we want.

---

to have unshakable confidence in our salvation, we must be sure it is built on the solid rock of God's truth, which will last throughout eternity. "Heaven and earth will pass away, but my words will not pass away" (Matthew 24:35). God's eternal, infallible, and inerrant Word is the only sure foundation for doubt-proof confidence. Beauty may be in the eye of the beholder, but salvation is not. God's Word, not human opinions or speculations, provides the knowledge we need for the salvation we claim and the confidence we want.

The Bible tells us that God sets the parameters of salvation and eternal life. The Bible is clear about salvation. We can't earn it, bargain for it, or buy it. We don't deserve it, can't inherit it, and won't receive it just because we believe in it. It is God who determines both the meaning and the means of salvation.

Salvation is too important to be ignored, misunderstood, or confused about it. So, we need a clear picture of what the Bible says about it.

A clear picture can be ours, but it takes revelation on God's part and effort on our part. God has and will continue to do His part, but we must do our part. Let me explain. We all begin our spiritual journey, lost and blind. The Bible says:

> And even if our gospel is veiled, it is veiled to those who are perishing. 4 In their case the god of this world has blinded the minds of the unbelievers, to keep them from seeing the light of the gospel of the glory of Christ, who is the image of God. (2 Corinthians 4:3-4)

However, after God opens our eyes to the truth of the gospel and saves us, we still have to deal with a sinful world and our flesh. The two work together to mar our image and understanding of God and our salvation. Therefore, we need ongoing spiritual revitalizing as long as we are in this world and our fleshly bodies.

Think of it this way. I can see the words of this book as I type it because I did my part, meaning I made an appointment and went to an ophthalmologist several years ago. He examined my eyes and prescribed glasses for me, so he did his part. However, if I want to see clearly, in between my visits to him, I must regularly clean off the dust and smudges that collect on my lenses.

To see spiritually, we don't need an ophthalmologist. We need an all-sufficient God. God enables us to see our sinfulness and its solution, which is Jesus. It is God who convicts us of our sinfulness and gives us the faith to believe in Jesus. If God doesn't open our eyes, we are spiritually blind to the things of God and the Word of God. But even after God does His part (saves us), we must continue doing our part. We must occasionally remove misconceptions and unbiblical views that our minds unknowingly collect from the voices and images around us. If we don't, our vision of God and understanding of His salvation become marred. When a less than clear picture emerges, it allows others (Satan, the world, and the flesh) to paint a different view, a distorted one of God and His salvation.

We can use a lens cleaning cloth for our glasses, but we need the washing of His Word (see Ephesians 5:26) for our minds. When we go back to the Bible (our part), God then uses

His Word to paint a clear picture of Himself, His amazing grace, and His salvation in our minds (again His part). This process is vital. Furthermore, we can have unshakable confidence in our salvation by maintaining a clear picture of it. However, this requires removing any misconceptions and getting equipped with the evidence that supports them. And, having a clear picture of salvation also requires knowing the essentials of salvation.

Chapter 7:
The Essentials

After twenty-seven years of living in a parsonage, my family and I began searching for our own home with the church's permission. However, after several months of searching, I got discouraged. Every home we checked out had positives and negatives. The idea of investing so much in a home with negatives created a cloud of despair for me. I just couldn't settle for a house that was not very close to my idea of a dream home. Therefore, my family and I discussed and came up with a list (unwritten) of essentials that our new home had to have to be our dream home.

I wanted natural gas, a location not too far from the church I pastor, a basement, a yard of decent size, a two-car attached garage. And, of course, it had to be one that we could afford. My two college kids needed fast-speed internet and bedrooms that were much bigger than a large closet (essential for my son, who had lived his entire life [19 years] in such a room). My wife wanted a basement plus a garden spot, lots of kitchen cabinets, and large closets. And we all wanted a fireplace.

After many hours of web searching and onsite visits, we stumbled on, or should I say, God providentially guided us to a home for sale by the owner. It was love at first sight. It had all the essentials, all that we had dreamed about, longed for, and then some. We felt God had done abundantly more than we had asked. Oh, it had two fireplaces. (I love fireplaces.)

Essentials are not only crucial in buying a house; they are critical in God's saving plan. The Bible says that Jesus came to save the lost. "For the Son of Man came to seek and to save the lost" (Luke 19:10). The act of salvation involves a minimum of three essentials. However, we need to understand the word essential before looking at them. It means it is impossible to remove it without destroying the object. For our new home to be our dream home, it had to have all the essentials on our list. Otherwise, it is no longer our dream home. Therefore, if our salvation is to be sure and steadfast, it must have the following essentials.

God is Essential

"In the beginning, God created the heavens and the earth" (Genesis 1:1). If there is no God, there would be no heaven, no eternal life, no salvation, and no spiritual meaning to life. However, the good news is that God exists, and, of course, He's essential to all of the above. Therefore, we begin with God because true spirituality, salvation, and eternal life depend on God.

Although we are born with a bent toward believing in God, not just any god will do. Unfortunately, our desire to believe in God can create a god out of anything. So, when two people converse about God, they may not be speaking about the same God but merely their perception of God.

Many have faith in a generic god. While a generic brand of medicine can save you money, a generic version of god can cost you everything. Although many toss the word *god* around, we should not conclude they are referring to the God of the Bible. Many so-called gods are worshiped, but they fail to match the God of the Bible.

The Bible tells us He is the God of Creation. He is *Elohim,* God almighty, who has the power and authority to save and condemn. It also tells us He is holy and just, and because He is holy, He requires all sin be punished. Thus, there is a need for salvation.

His holiness cannot ignore our sin. However, His love cannot turn its back on us. In His wisdom, God created a plan to redeem us, to reconnect with us. He devised a means to satisfy the demands of His holiness and grant the desires of His love. He provided a substitute, someone who was sinless yet willing to die for our sins. He sent Jesus Christ, the Savior of the world.

Although the God of the Bible is truly unique, why should we choose Him above all the other so-called gods? How about the fact that He has proven Himself? Those who have put their trust in Him and committed their lives to Him have found that He fulfills all the Bible describes Him to be. However, has He given us reasons to choose Him over other supposed gods?

> In His wisdom, God created a plan to redeem us, to reconnect with us. He devised a means to satisfy the demands of His holiness and grant the desires of His love.

The Bible claims to be the product of God:

> All Scripture is breathed out by God and
> profitable for teaching, for reproof, for
> correction, and for training in righteousness,
> 17 that the man of God may be complete,
> equipped for every good work. (2 Timothy
> 3:16–17)

Therefore, consider the following questions: Do these other gods provide a trustworthy track record? Do they offer a unified book complied of 66 different books, written by 40 different authors over 1,600 years and in three languages—Hebrew, Greek, and Aramaic—with a gap of over 400 years between the Old and New Testament? Yet, despite the time frame, multiple languages, and various authors, there is unity and consistency in doctrine and prophecy. Do the characteristics and attributes of these other gods match what is described in this unique book--the Bible? If the answer is no, and it will be, these truths help settle the debate.

The God of the Bible has given us an amazing book, unlike any other known to man. The Bible is unique, and so is God. He uses the Bible to reveal the purpose for His Son's coming and for dying on the cross.

It also clarifies that for our faith to be effective, for it to be saving faith, it must be directed toward and trusting in the One true God, the God of the Bible. It makes sense because eternal life can only come from an eternal, all-powerful God.

Those who reject God because they can't see Him, feel Him, or test Him, fail to take into account the nature of God. He is not a god of this world. He does not fit within the framework of man's understanding and knowledge. He can't be tested, confirmed, or verified in a laboratory. He is far above this world and undetectable to those in this world. He can only be known, and we can only have a relationship with Him if, and only if, He reveals Himself to us. He has done this through both general and special revelation.

General Revelation

God reveals Himself to all peoples of all lands through general revelation. We see God through His created order. A view of the heavens and the beauty of nature enables us to see the handiwork of God. So likewise, studying our universe allows us to know the order and logic that runs throughout it. King David said:

> The Heavens declare the glory of God, and the sky above proclaims his handiwork. Day to day pours out speech, and night to night reveals knowledge. (Psalm 19:1-2)

The apostle Paul writes:

> For his invisible attributes, namely, his eternal power and divine nature, have been clearly perceived, ever since the creation of the world,

in the things that have been made. So they are without excuse. (Romans 1:20)

Through general revelation, we see the necessity of a creator. If something exists, someone has to bring it to a state of existence. We naturally tend to believe in a creator since created things surround us. General revelation enables us to get a glimpse of the power and majesty of God. When we gaze at the vastness of the oceans, the beauty of snow-capped mountains, or take note of the two trillion galaxies in the observable universe, we find ourselves in awe.

In a limited sense, general revelation enables us to know we are subject to God. It may not be consciously thought out, but deep down, we know that if God created us and everything else, He determines how we and the world should function. But general revelation could never communicate our sinful condition, the need for a Savior, or God's plan of salvation. Therefore, God provided a detailed revelation, a special revelation.

Special Revelation

God's general revelation set the stage for His special revelation. His special revelation gives us a detailed message on sin and judgment, a clear understanding of the need for redemption, and how we can be redeemed. Apart from special revelation, we cannot know God personally. Apart from special revelation, we can never fully grasp God's hatred for sin and His wrath toward sinful humanity. Apart from special revelation, we could never know the power of God and the love of God and that they are available to us.

This power is essential because it enables us to resist sin and live a holy and God-honoring life. So, psalm 119:11 says, "I have stored up your word in my heart, that I might not sin against you." In chapter one of Ephesians, Paul says that we have the same power dwelling in us that raised Jesus from the grave (more about this in the chapter on the promises of God).

The knowledge we need to tap into the power we need is available because of the special revelation we have. But, of course, we must humbly look to the One who is the source of this power. This knowledge is excellent news because, with it, we can be victorious in our struggle with sin. We don't have to be jealous, envious, bitter, unforgiving, or vengeful. We can be Christ-like.

> Everyone needs salvation. We need it because the same God who makes salvation possible also makes it necessary.

It is also necessary to know and appreciate God's love for us, a love so great that He would sacrifice His own Son to pay the penalty for our sin. Through this special revelation, God reveals Himself more clearly to us. This special revelation comes through His Word---the Bible.

We know God exists through general and special revelation. Together, they enable us to see that our sins are real and salvation is essential.

They also help refute the arguments that God is a figment of man's imagination, an idea concocted to keep the masses in line, or a pie-in-the-sky for those who can't handle the adversities of life. But, when all is said and done, no amount of skepticism can do away with the presence and power of God, who exists and provides salvation to whoever will receive it.

Our next essential component is those who need salvation.

The Lost are Essential

If there were no lost—no unsaved people—no spiritually lacking people, there would be no need for salvation. However, the Bible is clear about this—everybody is lost. Everyone needs to connect spiritually to God. Everyone needs salvation. We need it because the same God who makes salvation possible also makes it necessary. He requires it because He is holy, and we are not. His holiness demands holiness; His standard is sinlessness because He is sinless. There is no sin, no darkness, no error, and no shortcomings in God. He is perfect, and we are not.

"Who is like you, majestic in holiness, awesome in glorious deeds, doing wonders*"* (Exodus 15:11)?

> And the four living creatures, each of them with six wings, are full of eyes all around and within, and day and night they never cease to say, 'Holy, holy, holy, is the Lord God Almighty, who was and is and is to come!' (Revelation 4:8)

Without holiness, we cannot have a relationship with God. Without holiness, we will not hear Jesus say, "Well done, good and faithful servant. You have been faithful over a little; I will set you over much. Enter into the joy of your master" (Matthew 25:21, 23). Without holiness, we will never stroll over heaven or see the streets of gold.

But how can we get it? Holiness is not something that's in our nature. It can't be found in a gospel bookstore or bought on eBay. We may live good moral lives and treat others (most of the time) as we would like them to treat us, but holy, we are not. We have evil thoughts, do bad things, and make poor decisions. We have emotional moments that produce sinful attitudes, bad words, and hurtful actions.

An honest look in the mirror produces a sense of hopelessness, the kind the Israelites felt at the Red Sea. After being set free from Egyptian bondage, they found themselves trapped with the Red Sea before them, mountains on either side of them, and Pharaoh's army approaching them. With the roar and thunder of Pharaoh's chariots approaching, hope faded from their minds, and fear gripped their hearts. But then God delivered them. The same is true for us. With every remembrance of passages like Hebrews 12:14, the hope of heaven is soon replaced by the fear of death and a vision of hell. "Strive for peace with everyone, and for the holiness without

> We may live good moral lives and treat others (most of the time) as we would like them to treat us, but holy, we are not.

which no one will see the Lord" (Hebrews 12:14). But just as God delivered the Israelites from their hopeless state, so can He deliver us from our unholy state.

However, we must realize our spiritual state before our deliverance can occur. After all, we are blind to our spiritual condition and need for salvation, which means God must get our attention and reveal our state to us. Thankfully, His Spirit convicts and His love draws.

In His wisdom, He gave us His Word. On the one hand, it destroys any false hope we might have of entering heaven through our goodness and holiness; while also providing God's hope and holiness to us. On the other hand, He has also sent His Spirit to convict (convince) us of our need for salvation and provide us with the faith needed to trust His Son for our forgiveness. Thankfully, God loved us enough to reach out to us and send His Son to die for us.

When criticized by the Pharisees for mingling with sinners and tax collectors, Jesus pointed out that it was for the sinners that He came into the world.

> But when he heard it, he said, 'Those who are well have no need of a physician, but those who are sick. 13 Go and learn what this means, 'I desire mercy, and not sacrifice.' For I came not to call the righteous, but sinners. (Matthew 9:12-13)

God loves the lost, and He came to save the lost. We are lost until, by God's grace, He saves us. But does God's love and

> As it is written: "None is righteous, no, not one;
> 11 no one understands; no one seeks for God. 12
> All have turned aside; together they have
> become worthless; no one does good, not even
> one." (Romans 3:10-12)

Christ's sacrifice means everyone will be saved? The Bible clearly says no. The most well-known verse in the Bible, John 3:16, points this out. It reads, "For God so loved the world, that he gave his only Son, that whoever believes in him should not perish but have eternal life." Salvation is dependent on believing—trusting in Christ. Salvation requires the work of Christ and faith on the part of the believer.

Furthermore, the increasingly accepted belief of the post-modern generation is that all religions are true and everyone is heaven-bound. This, too, is false. If it was true, there would be no need for salvation. If it was true, there would be no need for a Savior. If it was true, there would be no need for God to send His Son and no need for Christ to have suffered and died on the cross. If it was true, God would be a liar, Jesus' death would have been a waste, and this book would be pointless.

But it's not true. God requires holiness, and, unfortunately, all humanity has sinned and come short of God's standard of holiness. "As it is written: None is righteous, no, not one; 11 no one understands; no one seeks for God. 12 All have turned aside; together they have become worthless; no one does good, not even one" (Romans 3:10-12).

We are lost—cut off from God—because of our sins, but God's love can save us. We are not holy, but Christ is holy. We cannot save ourselves, but Christ can save us. His holiness becomes our holiness. His righteousness becomes our righteousness. Therefore, Christ is essential to biblical salvation.

Christ is Essential

To satisfy the demands of God's holiness and provide for man's salvation, God has provided a means to accommodate both. Christ is that means. He is the key to salvation and God's holy requirements. Salvation is only possible because of Christ and only received through repentance and faith in Christ. "And there is salvation in no one else, for there is no other name under heaven given among men by which we must be saved" (Acts 4:12). "I am the way, and the truth, and the life. No one comes to the Father except through me" (John 14:6). "And this is the testimony, that God gave us eternal life, and this life is in his Son. 12 Whoever has the Son has life; whoever does not have the Son of God does not have life" (1 John 5:11-12).

> Salvation is only possible because of Christ and can only be obtained through repentance and faith in Christ.

In Christ, we can have a *know-so* relationship with God. It is through Christ that we can obtain true spirituality. He came into this world to be our mediator, our advocate. He did what no one else could do. He paid the price for our sins. He provided a bridge to bring us back to God. He makes possible a restored relationship with God. "For Christ also suffered once for sins, the righteous for the unrighteous, that he might bring us to God, being put to death in the flesh but made alive in the spirit" (1 Peter 3:18).

The first Adam brought sin into the world, destroying our relationship with God; the second Adam, Christ, died for the world's sins and brought restoration to us. "For if, because of one man's trespass, death reigned through that one man, much more will those who receive the abundance of grace and the free gift of righteousness reign in life through the one man Jesus Christ" (Romans 5:17).

This restored relationship means we have eternal life with God, both of which are made possible by Christ. He is the doorway by which we enter this restored relationship. Christ saves us from the power of sin, the penalty of sin, and the wrath of God.

I have a lot of keys on my key chain. Many of them look alike, but only one will open the door to my house. The world is full of religions and religious leaders. In some ways, they may appear similar in practice and doctrine, but only Christ provides the key to heaven. Only Christ can provide the pathway to true spirituality. We cannot have salvation apart from Christ. He provides the means, and He is the key to it. I know of no church or denomination that denies the need for belief in Christ for salvation (although there may be some).

Unfortunately, many don't understand that salvation in Christ means nothing less than:

(1) Believing Jesus existed and is the Son of God.

(2) Accepting that He lived a perfect life, died a sacrificial death, and was raised from the dead by God the Father.

(3) Repenting and putting one's faith in Christ by committing one's life to Christ and submitting to His authority and His Word.

True salvation in the biblical sense requires that God, who loves us, makes these three essentials real to us and in us. Salvation is a God thing. He does the saving by working in us and through us. He gives us an understanding of our lost state and provides us with the faith needed to believe in Christ.

Although God provides the truth we need, we must accept it and act on it. God's truths always lead to His Son. All spiritual journeys with heaven as the destination must travel a hard path that will converge at a narrow gate, and that gate is Jesus Christ.

> Enter by the narrow gate. For the gate is wide and the way is easy that leads to destruction, and those who enter by it are many. 14 For the gate is narrow and the way is hard that leads to life, and those who find it are few. (Matthew 7:13–14)

Chapter 8:
The Spiritual Benefits

We live in a *what's in it for me* culture. Our concern is for number one. Today's common philosophy is that it is more blessed to receive, and *I want my blessing now.* We view everything from a worldly standpoint. The primary question of the day is, "Can it help me financially, relationally, socially, or vocationally?" Yet, are we any different from Jesus's day? Were the people in the New Testament time just as self-centered and opportunistic? Yes, if the actions of Jesus' disciples are any sign.

In Matthew chapter 19, a wealthy young ruler came to Jesus, asking Him what he needed to inherit eternal life. When Jesus told him to sell all that he had and give it to the poor and follow him, the rich young ruler went away sad, and Peter went to Jesus with a question. Peter, speaking on behalf of himself and the other disciples, wanted to know what they would get from following Him since they had given up everything. Their focus was on getting, not giving, on putting money in their pockets, not leading sinners to the Savior. They were concerned with *what's in it for us?*

> Then Peter said in reply, "See, we have left
> everything and followed you. What then will we
> have?" 28 Jesus said to them, "Truly, I say to
> you, in the new world, when the Son of Man will
> sit on his glorious throne, you who have

followed me will also sit on twelve thrones, judging the twelve tribes of Israel. 29 And everyone who has left houses or brothers or sisters or father or mother or children or lands, for my name's sake, will receive a hundredfold and will inherit eternal life. (Matthew 19:27-29)

Instead of rebuking Peter for thinking, *what's in it for us?* He encouraged him and the other disciples with promises of positions and power. Also, He promised all of His followers' rewards of a hundredfold and eternal life once they arrive in His new kingdom. We see in this that it's okay to point out the rewards and benefits of heaven. Jesus uses our self-concern to put us on the right road to heaven. He wants us to know that the joys and rewards of heaven are worth the sacrifices and hardships of this life. However, in contrast to a health and wealth gospel, Jesus describes the difficulty of this life. Those who live a Christ-like life will have to travel, as He put it, a narrow road and through a straight gate with no place to lay your head.

However, a hard life should not surprise us. As long as we are down here, we are not home yet. Our good days are ahead of us. Our best life is not now but reserved for us in heaven, where our rewards await us. In the end, it will be worth it all— the old gospel song "When We All Get To Heaven" says it well.

Sing the wondrous love of Jesus
Sing His mercy and His grace

In the mansions bright and blessed
He'll prepare for us a place

When we all get to heaven
What a day of rejoicing that will be
When we all see Jesus
We'll sing and shout the victory

While we walk the pilgrim pathway
Clouds will overspread the sky
But when travelin' days are over
Not a shadow, not a sigh

When we all get to heaven
What a day of rejoicing that will be
When we all see Jesus
We'll sing and shout the victory

Onward to the prize before us
Soon his beauty we'll behold
Soon the pearly gates will open
We shall tread the streets of gold

When we all get to heaven
What a day of rejoicing that will be
When we all see Jesus
We'll sing and shout the victory

When we all see Jesus
We'll sing and shout the victory

In the second stanza, the author writes,

> While we walk the pilgrim pathway
> Clouds will overspread the sky
> But when travelin' days are over
> Not a shadow, not a sigh

> Whatever the cost, whatever the loss, whatever the pain, whatever the shame, it will be worth it all.

As we travel the pilgrim's pathway on earth, we will have clouds, storms, and tragedies that will overshadow our journey, but we have a home prepared for us in heaven. The author of this song understood the difficulties of this life very well. Eliza Edmunds Hewitt wrote this song in 1898. She was a devoted Christian who wanted to make a difference in the lives of children as a teacher. However, according to Robert J. Morgan, an unruly student slammed his slate across her, severely injuring her back. After enduring a heavy cast for six months, she could finally walk. Still, the after-effects of her injury prevented her from returning as a teacher. She then devoted herself to studying the Bible and hymn-writing.[8]

In Romans 8:18, the Bible states, "For I consider that the sufferings of this present time are not worth comparing with the glory that is to be revealed to us." So we, too, should consider the sufferings and heartaches of this life not worthy of being compared to the glories of heaven.

Whatever the cost, whatever the loss, whatever the pain, whatever the shame, it will be worth it all. Although some say that the devil is in the details, the joys of salvation are also in the details. Therefore, we need to consider the facts of our salvation. We begin with the benefits.

These heavenly benefits are eye-catching, soul gripping, and eternally satisfying. God designs them to appeal to a lost humanity. He knows what it takes to get our attention because He made us. He knew it would take a burning bush that didn't burn up for Moses, a storm at sea for Jonah, a talking donkey for Balaam, a dream for Joseph, a crowing rooster for Peter, and nail-scared hands for Thomas. And to a self-centered world, He promises eternal life and the immeasurable riches of heaven. God appeals to the sinful flesh of humanity to get the sinful flesh out of humanity. The lure of heavenly fortune catches the eye of many, and then the Holy Spirit points them to the pearl of great price—Jesus.

However, the benefits of salvation are not just for our heavenly home but also our journey along the way. Christ lived around thirty-three years on this planet so that He could experience all the hardships and sufferings of this world. He knows our needs, and through our ongoing relationship with Him, He provides all we need physically and spiritually.

God meets our needs through our salvation. Yet, although the word *salvation* is a frequently used word throughout Christianity, many do not understand the benefits associated with it?

Salvation implies someone or something being delivered or saved from something undesirable or dangerous. Biblical salvation includes being delivered from the consequences of sin, the power of sin, and the wrath of God. Those knowledgeable about Christianity know that its teachings stress salvation from hell; however, many do not understand other aspects or benefits of salvation.

The more we know of the benefits of salvation, the more we appreciate the value of salvation. But just what are they? Salvation delivers us from hell, the dominion of sin, and self. So we will first look at what it teaches about being saved from hell.

Saved from Hell

Biblical salvation involves being saved from a literal hell. Although the talk of hell is not politically or culturally well-received these days, it is necessary. The idea of hell, as well as many other spiritual matters, varies from person to person. For many, their concept of God, heaven, hell, and other spiritual issues are often nothing more than the products of their desires and longings. As a result, many reject the reality of hell, relegating it to horror movies and fantasy or a place reserved for ruthless people.

Although this book is about my spiritual journey and heaven as my destination, my understanding of God's salvation and hell's reality comes from the same place—God's infallible Word. If I or anyone

> Every sin is a rejection of God's authority over us, therefore, rebellion justifies His wrath and our punishment.

cannot believe all the teachings of God's Word, can we truly trust any of it? Either God has conveyed Himself and His thoughts to us, or He hasn't. If He hasn't, we have no sure direction and no sure hope of eternal life. But if He has, we can be saved, know that we are saved, enjoy being saved, and be sure of both a hell to shun and a heaven to gain.

To the surprise of many, hell is an actual place. How do I know this is true? Because Christ and His Word say so. Although we may deny it or ignore it, hell doesn't cease to exist because we don't like it. Hell is real, but it doesn't have to be a reality for us. Christ has provided the means to avoid it. Hell was initially designed for the angels who rebelled in heaven. "For God did not spare even the angels who sinned. He threw them into hell, in gloomy pits of darkness, where they are being held until the day of judgment" (2 Peter 2:4).

Unfortunately, humanity has rebelled against God. Therefore, hell became our destination. The problem many have with hell is that they categorize sins. They view people who live law-abiding lives and treat their family, friends, and neighbors well as not deserving of hell. They see it as a place reserved for the evil people of the world. They and we fail to realize that all sins, both small and large (small and large as to their impact and consequences), are offspring of the father of all sins, the sin of rebellion. Every sin is a rejection of God's authority over us; therefore, rebellion justifies His wrath and our punishment.

Jude warns us of the consequences of rebellion. He writes, "Woe to them! For they walked in the way of Cain and abandoned themselves for the sake of gain to Balaam's error and perished in Korah's rebellion" (Jude 11).

In Numbers 16:1-23, Korah instigated a rebellion against Moses' leadership. He and 250 other leaders of the nation challenged Moses, but in doing so, they also rebelled against God, who had put Moses in charge. In the end, God opened the earth and swallowed these leaders and all their families. There is no sin more damaging to our relationship with God than that of rebellion. It occurred first in the garden with Adam and Eve and continues to plague all of humanity since that day.

But that punishment doesn't have to take place. There is a way to escape it. Jesus emphasized the need to do whatever it takes to stay out of hell. By use of hyperbole (an exaggeration for effect). He states:

> And if your hand causes you to sin, cut it off. It is better for you to enter life crippled than with two hands to go to hell, to the unquenchable fire. [45]And if your foot causes you to sin, cut it off. It is better for you to enter life lame than with two feet to be thrown into hell. [47]And if

your eye causes you to sin, tear it out. It is better for you to enter the kingdom of God with one eye than with two eyes to be thrown into hell, [48]'where their worm does not die and the fire is not quenched.' (Mark 9:43-48)

He is not literally saying we should cut off our hand or foot or pluck out our eye. Instead, he says that we should take whatever extreme measures are necessary to avoid hell. Giving total control of one's life over to Jesus is an extreme measure but a necessary one.

Although all sin is a sin of rebellion, there's also the sin beneath the sin. When I heard this term used in a sermon by Tim Keller, pastor of the Redeemer Presbyterian Church in New York City, it stuck with me. What he was getting at is that beneath every sin, there is another sin. Although we might not view some sins as worthy of punishment or judgment, underneath every sin is found the greatest of all sins, the violation of the Great Commandment.

When Jesus was asked which of the commandments was the greatest, He provided us with a guiding principle for all our actions, which is love:

Teacher, which is the great commandment in the Law?" 37 And he said to him, "You shall love the Lord your God with all your heart and with all your soul and with all your mind. 38 This is the great and first commandment.39 And a second is like it: You shall love your neighbor as yourself. 40 On these two commandments depend all the Law and the Prophets. (Matthew 22:36-40)

When Jesus said on these two commandments depend on all the law and the prophets, He gave us the foundation for all relationships, which is the foundation of love. Therefore, any act or thought that violates the principle of love is a sin that violates the greatest of all commandments, the commandments to love God and others. For instance, if I lie about someone, I sin against God by lying, but I also sin by not loving the person I lied about or lie to. Likewise, if I steal something, I sin by stealing, but I also sin by not loving the one I stole from. James also points this out in his letter.

> If you really fulfill the royal law according to the Scripture, 'You shall love your neighbor as yourself,' you are doing well. 9 But if you show partiality, you are committing sin and are convicted by the law as transgressors. 10 For whoever keeps the whole law but fails in one point has become accountable for all of it. (James 2:8-10)

James says that the law of love is the royal or supreme law; thus, any act or thought that violates it is a royal sin. Therefore, any sin condemns us to hell because all sin is rebellion, as well as the breaking of God's royal law, the law of love.

However, because of Christ's love and sacrifice, we have the means to be saved from hell. But it doesn't stop there. God's love and salvation do more than protect us from hell; they also deliver us from sin's controlling power or dominion over us.

Saved from Sin's Power

The fog of American's spiritually prevents many from seeing an important truth. *Christians are saved from sin's power.* But, unfortunately, far too many live much as they did before professing faith in Christ. Studies reveal no discernible difference between the lifestyles of many professing Christians and non-Christians.

Such surveys have shown no discernible difference between the number of Christians and non-Christians who get divorced.

Although some divorces are justified and biblical, many are not. Christians should rarely find themselves faced with a troubled marriage that the grace of God and, with the help of others, cannot be restored. Do we not have a source of wisdom, love, and power non-Christians don't have?

Another sign of a lack of spiritual power and holiness among Christians is cohabitation before marriage. Unfortunately, the sinfulness of cohabitation has been flushed down the toilet by a world that worships sex. All the while, the church is silent.

What is happening? Why is the Bible losing its authority among Christians? How can believers be salt and light in a dark and immoral world when many live contrary to the Bible's teachings? They can't. The Bible is clear about salvation delivering us from the power of sin. "Therefore, if anyone is in Christ, he is a new creation. The old has passed away; behold, the new has come" (2 Corinthians 5:17).

> When we continue to live like the world, after claiming to receive Jesus as Savior, something is not right.

And to further clarify God's stand on morality, Peter writes:

> As obedient children, do not be conformed to the passions of your former ignorance, [15] but as he who called you is holy, you also be holy in all your conduct, [16] since it is written, 'You shall be holy, for I am holy.' (1 Peter 1:14-17)

When we continue to live like the world, after claiming to receive Jesus as Savior, something is not right. As my aunt Irene and aunt Artie used to say, "There's a skunk in the woodpile."

A salvation that doesn't save us from the dominating power of sin gives evidence that there's a skunk in the woodpile. Something just doesn't smell right. What's wrong? What's the answer?

Deception! Deception occurs among Christians and non-Christians. Deception can and has worked its magic on the minds of many, causing them to see no wrong in an activity that the Bible clearly labels as sinful. Deception can cause us to believe we are saved when we are not. The spiritual fog that engulfs our churches fills the airwaves and is found in the tweets and blogs of the internet, blinds us to the truth of God's Word. What reality are we blinded to? The people of God have power from God to live a life that honors God.

Can a person be saved yet continue to live a life of sin? I'm sure you've already guessed it; the Bible says no. One of the benefits of salvation is that it delivers us from a life of sin— from sin's domineering power. Does this mean that true Christians will never sin? Of course not. God's salvation doesn't make us perfect, at least not in this world. We live in a sinful world, and the flesh is still with us, but once we receive Christ, we have a power from on high.

Although we have the power, we don't automatically have the knowledge or wisdom to use it. So we are instructed to grow in the grace and knowledge of our Lord and Savior. Although it is a fact that Christians sin and immature Christians sin more often, it is not true that a follower of Christ can live in a state of consistent and willful sin. A salvation that delivers us from hell can deliver us from sin's power.

Having said this, can a person struggle with a particular sin? Absolutely. But the keyword is *struggle.* If Christ is in us, we can never be comfortable living in ongoing sin. If Christ is in us, we may struggle with sin and be defeated by sin. Still, we will never surrender to sin and most definitely not justify it, accommodate it, and be content with it.

An absence of holiness and a willful persistence in sin shows a lack of Christ. This kind of lifestyle and attitude is typical of an unregenerate state. Such a person cannot confidently or biblically claim to be saved or expect to enter heaven's gates. Any so-called salvation that cannot deliver us from sin's power is a counterfeit. The spiritual fog is thick with this truth. It often blinds us to the reality of sin and the ability of Christ to deliver us from evil. It clouds our minds and weakens our will. It allows us to make excuses and encourages us to reinterpret the Scriptures to accommodate sin and its pleasures.

Amid this fog, a truth needs to be considered. Sometimes the issue is not Christians struggling with sin, which they cannot overcome, but a sinner struggling with Christianity, which is still at arm's length. Satan is a master deceiver. Unfortunately, much of what I see today is a form of Christianity that doesn't meet the criteria of biblical Christianity. Many are embracing a form of *moralistic therapeutic deism,* a term coined by sociologist Christian Smith. This counterfeit Christianity often embraces moral principles found in the Bible. Still, it allows a person to be disconnected from God while viewing Him as a 24/7 butler and therapist. However, the one thing this counterfeit doesn't do is confront and condemn sin.

> Any so-called salvation that doesn't deliver us from sin's power is a counterfeit.

We need to consider two questions in light of Christians who brazenly sin. First, can a Christian

116

continue in sin? But, of course, the answer is no. Next, can a sinner (one who continues to sin) yet, be saved? And the answer is yes. A sinner can be saved if they realize they are not saved. Suppose we can get past decades of spiritual fog. In that case, we will see clearly that deliverance from sin's controlling power is one benefit of salvation. "What shall we say then? Are we to continue in sin that grace may abound? By no means! How can we who died to sin still live in it" (Romans 6:1-2)?

> So you also must consider yourselves dead to sin and alive to God in Christ Jesus. 12 Let not sin therefore reign in your mortal bodies, to make you obey their passions. 13 Do not present your members to sin as instruments for unrighteousness, but present yourselves to God as those who have been brought from death to life, and your members to God as instruments for righteousness. 14 For sin will have no dominion over you, since you are not under law but under grace. (Romans 6:11-14)

"But now that you have been set free from sin and have become slaves of God, the fruit you get leads to sanctification and its end, eternal life" (Romans 6:22).

Those in Christ may choose to sin, but they do not have to sin. Before we came to Christ, we had no choice. We were under sin's power. But now that we are in Christ, and He is in us, we have been set free from the hold sin had on us. Although we are no longer physically bound by sin, we may be in mental bondage. It's like an elephant raised in a circus. Those of us who have been to a circus are often amazed at how a small metal

> We can be over-comers through Christ and His power, but only if we clearly understand what God says about sin, salvation, and the power and presence of the Holy Spirit.

stake driven in the ground can restrain a huge, mighty elephant. Why doesn't the elephant pull the stake out of the soil or break the chain or rope holding him to the stake? Why does he stay in bondage when he doesn't have to? Why doesn't he use the power he has to give him the freedom he desires?

The answer lies in his past. When he was small and weak, the rope or chain and stake were strong enough to hold him. As a baby elephant, he tried many times to break free, but to no avail. Thus, he came to believe he could never break free, so he stopped trying. Now, as an adult, he has the power to be free but stays in physical bondage because he's in mental bondage.

Christians can be free from sin's domineering influence. We can be over-comers through Christ and His power, but only if we clearly understand what God says about sin, salvation, and the power and presence of the Holy Spirit.

Christians must let go of their pre-Christian past. We must transform our thinking. We must allow God's Word to reshape our thoughts and give us the strength we need to live a holy and committed life for God's glory. "Do not be conformed to this world, but be transformed by the renewal of your mind, that by testing you may discern what is the will of God, what is good and acceptable and perfect" (Romans 12:2).

The Bible is clear. Christians have the power to be light to the world and salt to the earth, which is good news for a world filled with addictions, habits, insecurities, codependency, hatred, anger, violence, and sexual bondage. Never has our nation and churches needed more light and salt. The need for a moral and spiritual awakening is right here and right now.

Conservative political action groups may influence the laws of the land and the politicians on the hill, but they will never change the heart of a nation. To reverse the spiritual decline of our country and churches, we need biblically saved Christians, not professing Christians. Only the saved can tap into the power of God.

Therefore, we should expect holiness from those who claim to have a holy Jesus as Lord and Savior. We should expect it because they have received a new heart and new spirit that are sensitive to God's things, submissive to the Word of God, and empowered by the Spirit of God. We should expect it because Christ not only delivers us from sin's dominion, He also delivers us from self.

Delivered From Self

Put two small children in a room together and give each a different toy. Before long, each will want the toy the other has. It's in our genes to be selfish and self-focused. However, it is becoming fashionable among adults in today's society (as long as your selfishness doesn't impede my selfishness). Violating the rights of others and breaking the laws of the land is never right. Furthermore, good motives, just causes, or unfair practices of the past do not justify selfish actions, ignoring the rights of others, and breaking the laws of the land. Two wrongs never make for right, and they never will.

Our nation has become the world's capital of individual freedoms and personal rights. Each man or woman is their king or queen who sets the rules on how they will live and want to be treated.

Biblical salvation, however, delivers us from this mindset. Salvation gives us a new focus and a new direction. The throne that self once ruled from is now seated by the Savior, who is Lord of all. The power and desire to live for others comes from the One who died for others. The saved sacrifices for the good of others but do not demand that others do the same for them. They will not bully and badger people in the name of their so-called just cause, for doing so promotes the very thing they say they are against—bullies and injustice. We must show Christ's love to all people, especially to the neglected and underprivileged, but it will never seek the abuse of the privileged.

No good causes, excuses, or needs can justify putting self or anything else above the Savior. If He is Lord, He comes first in our lives. His Spirit within us makes it possible for us to live out His Will. It's insanity to think we can have two lords simultaneously--Jesus and self. Jesus said, "No servant can serve two masters, for either he will hate the one and love the other, or he will be devoted to the one and despise the other. You cannot serve God and money" (Luke 16:13). We must love all people, regardless of their skin color, political beliefs, or religious affiliations. And we must be a servant to all.

But does this mean Christians will not have their self-serving moments or pity parties? Of course not. Christians are still human. There will be times when our words or actions are flavored with selfishness. But it will not control our lives. We will not live under its power because becoming a Christian is more than embracing a new belief system or turning over a new leaf. It's all about surrendering our hearts and lives to Jesus. He becomes our Lord, and we become His subjects. The apostle Paul stresses this to the Christians in Rome. He writes:

> When you were slaves of sin, you were free in regard to righteousness. [21]But what fruit were you getting at that time from the things of which you are now ashamed? The end of those things is death. [22]But now that you have been set free from sin and have become slaves of God, the fruit you get leads to sanctification and its end, eternal life. [23]For the wages of sin is death, but the free gift of God is eternal life in Christ Jesus our Lord. (Romans 6:20-23)

When Paul says we've been set free from sin, he doesn't mean we are free from sin's presence or sin's influence, but we are free from its control. We are free from it because we have a new master. We have embraced the lordship of Jesus Christ.

Salvation involves letting go of our rights. His Word, not our desires, becomes the authority over our lives. We willingly surrender our freedoms because of our faith in Christ, which is an all-compassing faith. It is not just faith in His saving power

> Anything less than lordship salvation (salvation that accepts Christ's lordship over our lives) is not biblical salvation.

but also in His knowledge of what is best for us. We trust His love to want what is best for us and His ability to accomplish it; therefore, we surrender all to Jesus.

Anything less than lordship salvation (salvation that accepts Christ's lordship over our lives) is not biblical salvation. It thus cannot save. Moreover, claiming to receive Christ as Savior but not as Lord disagrees with the Bible's presentation of salvation. The whole idea of salvation is that the Spirit of God has entered us and regenerated us. We become new creatures., creatures of faith. We either experience complete regeneration or no regeneration.

Consequently, His Word has the final say about dating, divorce, and decisions about our body, spouse, children, friends, fellow-workers, employers, country, environment, church workings, money, etc. What we want and desire can no longer be the driving force in our lives as in times past.

Although we are not perfect and cannot submit ideally to His Lordship, our love for Jesus will be a reality in our lives. His Word will be the apple of our eye and the guidebook for our lives. If it is not, there is something very wrong with our so-called salvation.

> And everyone who hears these words of mine and does not do them will be like a foolish man who built his house on the sand. 27 And the rain fell, and the floods came, and the winds blew and beat against that house, and it fell, and great was the fall of it. (Matthew 7:26-27)

True salvation delivers us from ongoing selfishness and self-centeredness. Thus, it has been rightly called radical salvation. It is so extreme that Jesus describes it as being born again (see John 3:5).

The Apostle Paul confirmed the radicalness of it when he wrote: "Therefore, if anyone is in Christ, he is a new creation. The old has passed away; behold, the new has come" (2 Corinthians 5:17).

The old person, the unsaved, lives according to the desires of the flesh. They do it their way, but this is not the way of the new creation. Therefore, if any man or woman is in Christ, they must become new creatures, for the old person is gone. We are now set free to live for God and others. We can now follow the example that Jesus set for us. "For even the Son of Man came not to be served but to serve, and to give his life as a ransom for many" (Mark 10:45).

We must become other-minded instead of self-focused, self-centered, and self-serving.

Delivered from Discontentment

> It is Christ, not new careers, new jobs, new houses, or new spouses that can provide lasting zest in our life, joy in our hearts, and contentment in our souls.

One benefit of salvation that I realized from personal experience is that it gives us meaning and purpose in life, which, in turn, gives us contentment. Although we are created for a meaningful relationship with God, sin destroyed it.

Thus, we futilely try to fill this void. Careers, sex, drugs, alcohol, fame, achievements, money, etc., may temporarily fill it, but only a restoration of a relationship with God can permanently satisfy it. We are never wholly content in life until our lives are centered on Christ.

Christ, not causes, campaigns, or crusades, gives us a sense of purpose and fulfillment. It is Christ, not new careers, new jobs, new houses, or new spouses, that provide lasting zest in our life, joy in our hearts, and contentment in our souls.

Many biblical verses stress that if we have Christ, we have all that we need:

For in him all the fullness of God was pleased to dwell, 20 and through him to reconcile to himself all things, whether on earth or in heaven, making peace by the blood of his cross. (Colossians 1:19-20)

For in him the whole fullness of deity dwells bodily, and you have been filled in him, who is the head of all rule and authority. (Colossians 2:10)

For the sake of Christ, then, I am content with weaknesses, insults, hardships, persecutions, and calamities. For when I am weak, then I am strong. (2 Corinthians 12:10)

But haven't other Christians and we experienced times of discontentment, whether in our marriages, jobs, or life in general? The answer is yes. Believers in Christ are still emotional creatures. The difference is that discontent doesn't have to fill our lives, rule our hearts, or determine our decisions. Salvation enables us to have victory, but it does not guarantee it. Victory requires focusing on Christ and letting Him fill us with His presence. The key is His presence; it replaces discontent with contentment, discouragement with encouragement, purposelessness with purpose and meaning.

My journey included a stage in my life where I was single, in my late twenties, and without warning, a heavy fog of discontentment descended on me. I watched my older brother get married, then my younger brother, and then my sister, ten years my junior. I began to wonder, would I ever find someone with which to share my life? Would I ever have children? The discontentment came without warning, and disillusionment and depression grew out of it. Although I had a great job and wonderful parents, life became more unsatisfying. Thankfully, I discovered that discontentment and discouragement were inconsistent with being a child of God. The Bible is clear. Christ is the key to contentment, not worldly possessions, not youth and health, and not even a spouse and family.

I was determined to be more than a conqueror through Christ. Therefore, whenever I became discouraged, depressed, or just filled with melancholy, I'd take a walk down a side road near my home. I would go equipped with selected memorized verses from the Bible and my pet poodle on a leash. As we walked and talked (my poodle just listened), I quoted my Bible verses over and over, sung parts of gospel songs, and took notice of God's presence in the beauty of His creation. My poodle and I would do this for a couple of miles and then head back home.

When you are full of Christ, mentally and emotionally, you are full of His presence, His peace, His contentment, and His joy. One verse that held special significance for me was Matthew 6:33. "But seek first the kingdom of God and his righteousness, and all these things will be added to you."

By putting Him first and trusting Him completely, I had the promise of receiving all I needed, not necessarily everything I wanted. But I also discovered that I already had everything I needed by putting Him first, for He is all we need.

Chapter 9:
The Spiritual Effects

We live in a world of cause and effect. For every cause, there is an effect. For every effect, there is a cause. After accepting and receiving Christ as Lord and Savior, what can a person expect? What kind of effect does salvation have on us? Although we've already looked at some of the salvational results, we need to examine specific detailed effects when one experiences God's saving grace.

When a person receives Christ as Lord, change happens. It may be dramatic and visible to others or more of an internal change. It depends on where a person is morally, emotionally, and socially when they receive Christ. However, there will be a dramatic internal change even when there is no immediate observable change.

Eventually, this change will show up in one's actions and attitudes. By recognizing these changes and realizing they are the products of salvation, the believer is assured of their salvation. These powerful effects (transitions) are the by-products of spiritual regeneration.

> Regeneration is the work the Holy Spirit accomplishes in every believer.

He saved us, not because of works done by us in righteousness, but according to his own mercy, by the washing of regeneration and renewal of the Holy Spirit. (Titus 3:5)

Regeneration produces change. These changes are so radical that the Bible uses such terms as *born again, born of God,* and *born of the Spirit.* (See John 3:3-13; 1 John 3:9; 4:7; 5:1; 1 Peter 1:23). Regeneration is the work the Holy Spirit accomplishes in every believer.

Salvation is and must be more than a religious, emotional experience. Although emotions can create a strong desire to change, they cannot provide the power for lasting change. For example, we may become emotionally excited in a worship service, resulting in a desire to change how we live. Still, the ability to do so is just not there. Sometimes we are motivated by a tragedy or life-changing event, so we determine that we will be different and live differently. Still, we eventually return to our old state. We must realize that salvation is much more than emotions and self-determination. Regardless of what creates a desire for change, most people need help to effect radical personal transformation. Biblical salvation is not about turning over a new leaf, doing better, or becoming a better version of the old self. Instead, it's about being regenerated by the Spirit of God. The following are some of the more dramatic effects produced in a believer.

New Heart

The heart is a vital organ in the human body. It provides the energy needed to push life-giving blood throughout our bodies.

However, the new heart that we receive when we experience the new birth has nothing to do with the organ known as the heart. But, the new heart received at the time of our spiritual rebirth is just as essential to our spiritual life as the physical heart is to our physical life. The Bible portrays the heart as the seat of our personality. It's what guides us and controls us. It's where our desires come from. It's the real us.

> A new heart is an absolute necessity in the new birth. It is essential for knowing and loving God. It's vital to be changed by God and become an instrument of change for God.

The world has one view of the heart, and God has another. Songs that fill the airways and romance novels that fill the bookshelves tell us to follow our hearts, listen to our hearts, and trust our hearts, but God says the opposite. The Bible says the unsaved heart is wicked above all things because we are naturally wicked. "The heart is deceitful above all things, and desperately sick; who can understand it" (Jeremiah 17:9)?

An unregenerate heart is self-focused; it seeks the things of this world, is self-pleasing, self-loving, and often self-destructive. It desires pleasures to please the flesh and turns to alcohol and drugs to ease the pain. In the end, it takes us down the wide road and through the broad gate that leads to a dead end.

An unregenerate heart is incomplete. It cannot properly love God or others. What I mean by properly is that it can't love unconditionally. Since we are made in God's image, we were initially equipped to love like God, but sin has so marred us that our love is far from what it should be and could be.

An unregenerate heart is selfish, and the type of love it produces is primarily self-serving and self-accommodating. It's a love that demands to be loved back, or else it will stop loving, which is not God's kind of love. God's love is unconditional. It's a love that will love others without expecting or demanding love. It will even love our enemies. Jesus made this clear in His Sermon on the Mount:

> You have heard the law that says, 'Love your neighbor' and hate your enemy. 44 But I say, love your enemies! Pray for those who persecute you! 45 In that way, you will be acting as true children of your Father in heaven. For he gives his sunlight to both the evil and the good, and he sends rain on the just and the unjust alike. 46 If you love only those who love you, what reward is there for that? Even corrupt tax collectors do that much. 47 If you are kind only to your friends, how are you different from anyone else? Even pagans do that. 48 But you are to be perfect, even as your Father in heaven is perfect. (Matthew 5:43-48)

The new heart takes our love up a holy notch. It enables us to love more like God. We can love without expectations, recognition, or gratitude. We can love those who hate us and mistreat us. We can love those who are unlovable, disgusting, foulmouthed, unconventional, unconverted, and who reject traditional gender roles and sexual norms. We can even love those who deny the existence of God.

We can love them because God loves them, and we have the nature of God within us. The Holy Spirit regenerates our hearts (the real us) and fills us with His love. Thus, when God saves us, He gives us a new heart. "I will give them a heart to know that I am the Lord" (Jeremiah 24:7).

There are no words that can adequately describe the importance of this benefit. A new heart is an absolute necessity in the new birth. It is essential for knowing and loving God. It's vital to be changed by God and become an instrument of change for God. It's necessary to be a light to the world and salt to the earth. It's essential if our decision for Christ is to be followed by a desire to follow Christ.

In the early stages of a baby's development, its heart is already formed and beating (within 5-6 weeks of conception). The new birth begins with a new heart. We are born again from the inside out. God gives us a new heart, and the new heart gives us a new look, a new perspective, new desires, a new life, and a new love for God and others.

One of my favorite verses is Psalm 37:4, "Delight yourself in the Lord, and he will give you the desires of your heart." But does this mean I can desire anything, and God will give it as long as I delight in God? Yes, and no. God will not provide us with anything outside of His will, but if we have a new heart, this new heart, which will delight in God, will desire those things that are pleasing and honoring to God.

In times past, we loved the things of this world, but a new heart changed all of that. We seek the eternal, not the temporal. Our new heart hunger and thirsts for the things of God. Instead of the things of the world. The author of the book of Hebrews writes, "For here we have no lasting city, but we seek the city that is to come" (Hebrews 13:14).

This new heart longs for what we cannot see and will give up what we can see. It creates a desire for the heavenly city. Heaven becomes more than an alternative to hell; it becomes the focus of our hearts. Biblical salvation puts a new heart within us, and with it comes a new Spirit.

New Spirit

> And I will give you a new heart, and a new spirit
> I will put within you. And I will remove the heart
> of stone from your flesh and give you a heart of
> flesh. And I will put my Spirit within you, and
> cause you to walk in my statutes and be careful
> to obey my rules. (Ezekiel 36:26-27)

Before Jesus went away, He promised His disciples that the Holy Spirit would come. So, the Holy Spirit takes up residence in the believer at the moment of salvation. His role is to empower us, transform us, comfort us, and guide us. We

> We could no more live the Christian life without the Holy Spirit than we could live physically without oxygen.

could no more live the Christian life without the Holy Spirit than live physically without oxygen.

In a world filled with temptations, hardships, and an enemy called Satan (who seeks to destroy us), the Holy Spirit is necessary. He provides the power needed to live a Christ-honoring, sin-rejecting, God-focused, power-filled, and yet humble life.

> And I will ask the Father, and he will give you another Helper, to be with you forever, [17]even the Spirit of truth, whom the world cannot receive, because it neither sees him nor knows him. You know him, for he dwells with you and will be in you. [18]'I will not leave you as orphans; I will come to you.' (John 14:16-18)

Believers have the promise of Christ's return, but until that day, Jesus provides us with a companion. The Holy Spirit is our helper. He empowers us to live out the teachings of Jesus.

The Greek word *paraklētos* in John 14:16 is translated *helper* in the English Standard translation and *comforter* in the King James translation.

He is our constant companion. He's there for us. He helps us in times of need. He comforts, supports, encourages, and strengthens all believers. We cannot live the Christian life without Him; we need His presence and power.

When I was small, my family would often go to the house where my mom grew up, and my mom's two unmarried sisters still lived. When one of my aunts would go out to the old board well to draw water, I'd always help. I could lower the empty board well bucket (a three ft. long slender bucket) into the well by myself with the help of a pulley and chain, but once it filled with water, it would become too heavy for me to pull up. It was then that my aunt would reach up and put her hands on the chain and pull with me. Together, we'd pull the bucket full of water out of the well.

When our lives become full of pain or heartache, or our faith becomes weak and wobbly, the Holy Spirit is there for us. He strengthens us. He supports us. He comforts us. When we need supernatural strength to love an abusive and harsh enemy, He provides it. When someone does cruel and hurtful things to us or those we love, He enables us to forgive them.

If we have a biblical salvation, we have the Spirit of God as our helper, which means we have at our disposal the power to obey Christ's commands. We can love the unlovable and forgive the unforgivable. We can honestly do His will because we have a heavenly helper (See Philippines 4:13).

New Life

Salvation not only puts a new heart and new spirit within us, but it also results in a new life for us, which is more than a new way of looking at things. The saved have new hope and new freedom to be what God desires of them and wants to accomplish in them and through them.

Before salvation, men and women are powerless against the ravages of sin, which can destroy relationships, marriages, and families. Sin can also shatter our dreams, darken our future, and drain our hopes. Biblical salvation, however, gives us a new life. It may not undo the mess we've made, take back the pain we've caused, or restore the lives we've destroyed, but it gives us hope of a new life. It enables us to put our past behind us. Once we are free from our past, we can chart a new path. God's forgiveness allows us to put the past behind us, look to the future before us, and make the most of our present.

Before the apostle Paul's conversion, he persecuted Christians and trusted his religious knowledge and works for his salvation. After his conversion, he became a new person. The past was behind him, and a new life was before him. The same is true for all who experience true salvation. Regeneration gives us a new heart, spirit, and a new life.

> Brothers, I do not consider that I have made it my own. But one thing I do: forgetting what lies behind and straining forward to what lies ahead, 14 I press on toward the goal for the prize of the upward call of God in Christ Jesus. (Philippians 3:13-14)

The possibility of a new life is good news that is greatly needed in today's world. Each year, the suicide rate in America increases among the old and young. Why? Are we not progressing as a society? Are we not the most prosperous nation in the world? Do we not have multiple televisions and cell phones filling our homes? Do we not have more ways to amuse ourselves, from Candy Crush to Murder Mayhem video games, to sports of every kind imaginable? Yet amid our amusements and techno-gadgets, our empty hearts are being filled with hopelessness.

God created us for relationships. We need meaningful relationships because we have a built-in need to feel valued. If we feel valued, we have a reason for existing and living. Gadgets and games can't give us value or meaning. The Holy Spirit reveals the love of God to us. He enables us to know that God loves and values us.

The Holy Spirit confirms that every believer is a child of God. As His children, we are members of His kingdom. As members of the kingdom, we have responsibilities; we have tasks to perform, giving us purpose. We are assigned a mission; to fulfill His will, communicate His message, and show His love.

As children of the King of kings, we have much to live for and rejoice about. We are valued by God, have received a mission from God, and have the promises of God. But, because of this new life, we also have new hope.

New Hope

Another result or effect of salvation is that it gives us new hope. Although hope, the state of desiring something with the expectation of obtaining it, is not something new, the hope that salvation provides is new.

Of course, we hope for many things and base them on many reasons. But then, who doesn't dream about obtaining better health, a better marriage, a better future, a better country, and a better world? But, unfortunately, our hopes often depend on new medicines, new surgery techniques, new technologies, and the newest political star of our party or mass movements in society. Unfortunately, when our hopes are dependent on human-based solutions, they are subject to the frailties and limitations of humanity. Consequently, they often don't materialize.

> But in Christ, our hope is different because it extends beyond this world and is not dependent on those of this world.

But in Christ, our hope is different because it extends beyond this world and is not dependent on those of this world. For instance, although death is a certainty, our new hope transforms it into an opportunity. Death is transformed into a doorway to a better life and a better world. The hope of heaven gives us the hope of victory over deadly or disabling diseases, unexpected tragedies, and devastating disasters, or painful losses. Why is this so? No matter how painful, discouraging, or disillusioning life may become, we know it's only temporary. We have a hope that can carry us through the valley of pain and death. We can endure to the end because our hope extends beyond the end. Our hope makes heaven real to us. It's a hope that circumstances, tragedies, or turmoil can't destroy. It's unshakable because it's anchored to God's eternal Word and made possible by Christ's sacrificial death and glorious resurrection.

> Blessed be the God and Father of our Lord Jesus Christ! According to his great mercy, he has caused us to be born again to a living hope through the resurrection of Jesus Christ from the dead, 4to an inheritance that is imperishable, undefiled, and unfading, kept in heaven for you. (1 Peter 1:3-4)

King David understood this hope. He fasted and prayed for his child's recovery when he was gravely ill. When the child died, his servants were afraid to tell him. He had been so distraught over the child's sickness; they feared he might harm himself now that the child was dead. But they didn't understand David's concept of the afterlife. After King David learned that the child had died, he cleaned up, put on a change of clothes, worshipped God, and then sat down to have a good meal. He had hoped that God would heal the child, but when He didn't, David still had a hope beyond the grave.

> [David] arose from the earth and washed and anointed himself and changed his clothes. And he went into the house of the LORD and

worshiped. He then went to his own house. And when he asked, they set food before him, and he ate. ²¹ Then his servants said to him, "What is this thing that you have done? You fasted and wept for the child while he was alive; but when the child died, you arose and ate food." ²² He said, "While the child was still alive, I fasted and wept, for I said, 'Who knows whether the LORD will be gracious to me, that the child may live?' ²³ But now he is dead. Why should I fast? Can I bring him back again? I shall go to him, but he will not return to me. (I Samuel 12:20-23)

He had hope of being reunited with his child in the afterlife. Every Christian has this new hope, one that transcends the grave.

Then I saw a new heaven and a new earth, for the first heaven and the first earth had passed away, and the sea was no more. 2 And I saw the holy city, new Jerusalem, coming down out of heaven from God, prepared as a bride adorned for her husband. 3 And I heard a loud voice from the throne saying, 'Behold, the dwelling place of God is with man. He will dwell with them, and they will be his people, and God himself will be with them as their God. 4 He will wipe away every tear from their eyes, and death shall be no more, neither shall there be mourning nor crying nor pain anymore, for the former things have passed away.' (Revelation 21:1-4)

This kind of hope sustains us when life disappoints us. It helps protect our hearts from becoming bitter when our health fails, our loved ones are taken from us, our friends turn against us, or our family abandons us. We believe that David wrote Psalm 27:10 during the time he was fleeing from King Saul. It reads, "For my father and my mother have forsaken me, but the Lord will take me in" (Psalm 27:10). His parents may have been afraid to take David in for fear of King Saul, but God would never forsake him.

I can relate to the hope that sustained David after the death of his child. Thankfully, our firstborn, Elizabeth, entered this world on Wednesday, May 8th, 1996. My dream had finally come true at 40. I was finally a dad. However, Elizabeth was more than my baby daughter. She was the fulfillment of the hopes, dreams, and prayers that had consumed my life for many years. She was five weeks premature and weighed 5 pounds and 6 ounces. According to the nurse, her heart rate was a little fast, but otherwise, everything looked okay. Then they took her to the Neo-natal ward for examination.

However, three hours later, the doctor and nurse from the Neo-natal intensive care ward entered my wife's room. The look on their faces said it all, but the words that followed made it real. *There's a problem,* said the doctor. She then explained that our daughter was hemorrhaging in the brain. They were giving her blood transfusions, as well as platelets, to increase the clotting factor. They had consulted another local hospital, but there was nothing more they could do. Finally, they told us we could visit Elizabeth after the shift change, around 8:30 p.m. Before they left, the doctor, hoping to prepare us for what was to come, said *it doesn't look good.*

At 8:30 p.m., we tried to enter the Neo-natal intensive care ward but were told to wait in the hallway. During the wait, the doctor who delivered our daughter showed up. They had called him in, but he didn't know the details. So he went into the Neo-natal intensive care ward to get more information. Shortly later, he and the doctor in charge of the intensive care unit emerged. They told us that the bleeding wasn't slowing down, there was nothing that could be done, and she would most likely not make it through the night. The two doctors then had everyone; my wife, her parents, and I hold hands, making a circle. With medical science powerless to stop or reverse my daughter's brain bleeding, these doctors looked to a greater power; they led us in prayer. After the prayer, they informed us that all the intensive care ward rules were suspended. We could stay with Elizabeth as long as we wished.

In the wee hours of the morning, my wife's parents took her back to her room to get some rest. The hospital chaplain stayed with me until some of my family members arrived from out of state. At one point, while sitting in a rocking chair with my daughter in my arms, I looked at the chaplain across from me and said, "I've heard it said that as long as there is life, there is hope." At which point, she interrupted with an affirmative. But then I said, "but I've discovered that as long as there is God, there is hope."

141

> When nothing in this world offers us hope, our relationship with Christ and knowledge of heaven can provide a hope like none other; a hope that can sustain us in our darkest hour.

I wanted her to know that although some say otherwise, this world is not all there is to life. However, with all the spiritual fog engulfing us, I can see why some might believe this life is it.

However, that night, while sitting in that Neo-natal Intensive Care ward, I had a hope that would not fade with the death of my daughter. I knew I would see her again, even if she didn't live through the night. Yes, everyone knows there is hope as long as there is life, but those in Christ know there is hope after this life.

Whether or not we realize it, this is the hope we are searching for on our spiritual journey. Thankfully, many are discovering this hope and seeing the light. They are being delivered from the fog of unbelief and deception and embracing Christ as Lord and Savior.

When nothing in this world offers us hope, our relationship with Christ and knowledge of heaven can provide hope like none other. This hope can sustain us in our darkest hour. It was true for me. In the wee hours of that morning, with darkness filling the sky above and my heart below, I prayed. I thanked God for giving me a daughter, regardless of how short her stay might be. I rejoiced over every minute I could hold her. Did I pray for her healing? Of course! Did I believe God could heal her? Absolutely. Was I sure He would? No. Amid my faith and doubt, I made some promises to God. I promised to give all the glory to Him should He heal her, but I also promised that should He take her home to heaven, I'd still love Him, trust Him, and serve Him. After finishing my prayer, God gave me peace that passes understanding.

> Do not be anxious about anything, but in everything by prayer and supplication with thanksgiving let your requests be made known to God. [7] And the peace of God, which surpasses all understanding, will guard your hearts and your minds in Christ Jesus. (Philippians 4:6-7)

To the amazement of the doctors and nurses, two and one-half weeks later, we took our daughter home. She is now 25 years old and excelled in sports and academics during her school years. She has just recently completed college with honors and a double major in math and computer science.

Sometimes God doesn't answer our prayers but gives us the grace to handle our disappointment. At other times, He answers our prayers, and we give Him thanks for doing it. But then, there are those times when God gives us more than we could ever imagine or hope. It's what He did for my family, and we praise Him for it.

> Now to him who is able to do far more abundantly than all that we ask or think,

according to the power at work within us, [21] to him be glory in the church and in Christ Jesus throughout all generations, forever and ever. Amen. (Ephesians 3:20-21)

> For I consider that the sufferings of this present time are not worth comparing with the glory that is to be revealed to us. (Romans 8:18)

This supernatural hope is vital. It enables us to view the injustices of this life from a better perspective. As great as the troubles and heartaches are down here, they are more than compensated for in our heavenly home. Does this mean we should not work to undo injustices? Of course not. However, it means that the things we cannot change, at least not in the short term, don't have to dampen our hope or diminish our joy. On the contrary, our best life, which awaits us in heaven, can be the focal point of our present life. We can suffer for Christ and others because we know a heavenly home that outshines this world is waiting for us.

In the previous chapter, we saw how the benefits of salvation help compensate for the hardships in this life. Well, no one knew this better than the apostle Paul. Although he had more than his share of heartaches and sufferings in this life, he kept His eyes fixed on heaven. "For I consider that the sufferings of this present time are not worth comparing with the glory that is to be revealed to us" (Romans 8:18).

But until God takes us home, we must reside in this pain-filled and temptation-plagued world. Unfortunately, while we are here, sin scars us. Although God's image is imprinted on us, sin scars some more than others. As a result, some effects or changes produced in us may be less evident in some than in others. Spiritual growth is the key to making these effects more apparent and prominent. Fortunately, we are motivated to grow spiritually. We receive new desires.

New Desires

Before salvation, we are prisoners of Satan. We don't have the strength or weapons needed to oppose him. We have no desire to be holy, live holy, or battle with the unholy. We are simply puppets under his control.

> And you were dead in the trespasses and sins 2 in which you once walked, following the course of this world, following the prince of the power of the air, the spirit that is now at work in the sons of disobedience—3 among whom we all once lived in the passions of our flesh, carrying out the desires of the body and the mind, and were by nature children of wrath, like the rest of mankind. (Ephesians 2:1-3)

The apostle Paul clarifies that we are dead to God before our salvation in the above passage. Therefore, we have no desire for God or the things of God. Instead, we solely focus our passions on our flesh, "carrying out the desires of the body and the mind" (Ephesians 2:3).

> The primary goal for the believer must be one of spiritual progress or growth, not spiritual perfection.

However, this all changes when salvation enters the picture. The Holy Spirit instills within us new desires. He gives us a hunger for God and His Word. It would have been great if, along with our salvation, God would have done away with our old spirit or sinful nature completely, but He didn't. Consequently, we will have to do battle with the flesh as long as we are in this world and have these fleshly bodies. And do battle, we will because we have new desires.

These desires motivate us to resist the devil and seek God's righteousness. We are saved sinners who desire to fight against sin and live for God. The flesh's influence or hold on us grows weaker as we grow spiritually.

The primary goal for the believer must be one of spiritual progress or growth, not spiritual perfection. This growth process is known as sanctification. We begin the Christian life as babes in Christ, but we must not remain spiritual babies. Growth is not an option; it is a necessity. The apostle Peter instructs his readers to desire or hunger for God's Word. "Like newborn infants, long for the pure spiritual milk, that by it you may grow up to salvation—³if indeed you have tasted that the Lord is good" (1 Peter 2:2-3).

Peter is saying that if we have tasted that the Lord is good, meaning if we have received Christ, then we should desire the Word of God like a baby craves milk. The key to our spiritual growth is to feed on God's Word. Therefore, we are given a desire for the pure spiritual milk of His Word. As a result, we become more like Christ, thus more holy in our thoughts and actions as we grow spiritually.

True salvation should produce a desire for His Word and be among His people. After all, we have one Lord, one faith, one Spirit, and one baptism (see Ephesians 4:4-6), all of which should draw us together as one body. Why is this vital? Although the Holy Spirit works directly in us, He also works through other believers to sanctify us.

The church is more than an option for believers; it is essential for our spiritual growth. Why do we need to grow spiritually? Well, God plans that we become like Christ. "For those whom he foreknew he also predestined to be conformed to the image of his Son, in order that he might be the firstborn among many brothers" (Romans 8:29).

Today we see many who claim to be Christians but have given up on the church. I believe we could trace this anomaly to one of two factors. First, could a lack of desire for the church be because of a lack of the Holy Spirit? Satan is masterful at deceiving us. Second, however, there could be another reason for this lack of desire. A combination of a previous bad church experience, plus a failure to understand the importance of the church, can water down our passion for the church.

The importance of the church cannot be overly emphasized. The church contributes to our spiritual growth. It does it through close relationships. We don't grow because we have our names on a church roll. It occurs when we agree to place ourselves willingly under the authority of His church and its leaders and have committed ourselves to one another within the church. The importance of committing ourselves to His church is emphasized in the book of Hebrews. In the following verse, we see that we help one another grow spiritually in the church's context.

> And let us consider how to stir up one another to love and good works, 25not neglecting to meet together, as is the habit of some, but encouraging one another, and all the more as you see the Day drawing near. (Hebrews 10:24-25)

Within the framework of the local church body, we are to think about how we can help believers with whom we worship and fellowship. How can we motivate them to grow in love and good works? It can't be done practically without being connected to and knowledgeable of those we are to help. God has designed the local church to help bring this about. An excellent book on how the church brings this about is *The Church and the Surprising Offense of God's Love* by Johnathan Leeman.

Thankfully, there will come a day when we will receive our glorified bodies, and the flesh will be no more. But until that time comes, we are to grow in the grace and knowledge of our Lord and Savior. Growth (sanctification) helps nullify the power and the hold the flesh has on us. As we grow spiritually, as we put off more of the old person and put on more of the new person, we become more like Jesus and grow more confident of our salvation.

> But that is not the way you learned Christ!—
> [21]assuming that you have heard about him and were taught in him, as the truth is in Jesus, [22]to put off your old self, which belongs to your former manner of life and is corrupt through deceitful desires, [23]and to be renewed in the spirit of your minds, [24]and to put on the new self, created after the likeness of God in true righteousness and holiness. (Ephesians 4:20-24)

In addition to the effects of salvation, the Word of God identifies vital telltale signs, evidence of our salvation. This evidence is necessary because when death comes for us, God wants us to be confident of our future destination, and we can be. We can have a *know-so* salvation that enables us to march peacefully and triumphantly through death's door, into heaven's light, and God's presence. Therefore, we need to examine the visible evidence of salvation.

Chapter 10:
The Visible Evidence

It was my first and, so far, last jury duty. As each case was brought before us, we listened and watched intently as the prosecution presented the evidence and then was refuted by the defense.

But in the end, the ball was in our court. We debated the evidence, reviewed the comments of the prosecution and the defense. If the

> How can we have assurance that when death comes for us, we will hear Christ say, "…Well done, good and faithful servant?" (Matthew 25:21)

evidence was clear enough, our verdict was easy enough. If it was vague and unimpressive, so were our convictions about the guilt or innocence of the one charged.

When death knocks at our door, will the evidence of our salvation be clear enough? Will it be strong enough? Will it be convincing enough to give us the peace we want, the certainty we need, concerning the home we desire? If so, we will experience death God's way. So His Word tells us that Christ died to deliver us from the fear of death.

> Since therefore the children share in flesh and blood, he himself likewise partook of the same things, that through death he might destroy the

> one who has the power of death, that is, the
> devil, [15] and deliver all those who through fear
> of death were subject to lifelong slavery.
> (Hebrews 2:14-15)

Christ conquered death; therefore, we should no longer fear it. Instead, we can walk boldly through death's door and into heaven's light. But this kind of confidence doesn't just happen because we accepted Christ as Lord and Savior.

What we need is solid, unshakable confidence in our salvation. We need to know without a doubt that we are one of God's children. But how? How can we know with absolute certainty that we are a child of God and joint-heirs with Christ? How can we have the assurance that when death comes for us, we will hear Christ say, "... Well done, good and faithful servant" (Mathew 25:21)?

Do we trust what others have said? Do we base it on beliefs that have no solid biblical foundation? Can a past decision for Christ give us confidence when faced with death? Can the effects of salvation, which we have looked at but are sometimes muted by the flesh, provide the assurance we need? My knowledge of the Scriptures and my experiences with dying saints tell me the answer is no to all the above. The key to our assurance lies solely with God's Word.

Biblical salvation is based solely on the Word of God, and so is the visible evidence of our salvation. But, unfortunately, the reality of our faith is on trial every day. Satan is the accuser of the brethren, and the world is constantly judging us. However, what matters most, when the time of our departure is at hand is what God says and what we know. Do we have the evidence that will effectively give us the assurance we need? Does it align with what God says?

Now let's go back to the courtroom where I was on jury duty. The spiritual realm is much like that courtroom. But instead of a jury of our peers, it's we who must be convinced. And we can be when the evidence matches the biblical threshold of proof. In that case, it can convince us beyond any reasonable doubt that we are saved and on our way to heaven. Then, instead of fearing death, we can enter it with complete peace and joyful expectation.

Unfortunately, deep down, we know that the opposite is also true. If we lack credible evidence, it shows a spiritual problem; the worst-case scenario being that we are not saved. Could this be why many never take time to examine themselves as the apostle Paul instructs in 2 Corinthians 13:5? Do we fear the worse, so we don't want to know the truth?

Galatians 5:22-23 tell us what to look for; we are to look for the fruit of the Spirit. Our spiritual fruit provides the evidence we need for the confidence we want concerning the salvation we claim. Therefore, examine the fruit carefully and honestly. Compare the fruit of the Spirit with your life. If you have and are bearing the fruit of the Spirit, rejoice. But if not, seek Christ. Seek His forgiveness and His grace.

Although I don't examine all of the fruit of the Spirit here, I do want to look at some outward signs of salvation that God provides throughout the Bible. Those who possess them can have the assurance needed to enjoy an abundant life and experience a fear-free, Christ-honoring death.

Forgiving Spirit

Christians can forgive those who wrong them because we have the spirit of Christ within us, which is a forgiving spirit. We are not to hold grudges, for we are instructed; no, we are *required* to forgive those who have harmed and mistreated us. "But if you do not forgive others their trespasses, neither will your Father forgive your trespasses" (Matthew 6:15).

Followers of Christ will forgive people for their trespasses because they have the power to forgive through the Holy Spirit. He is our strength and helper. We can and will forgive because we are servants of Christ. He is not just our Savior. He's our Lord; thus, we obey His command to forgive.

Peter asked Jesus how often we should forgive a brother who sins against us. Jesus replied, seventy times seven (see Matthew 18:21-22). This amount indicates an unlimited number. We need to understand that there is no limit to God's forgiveness, no limit to God's grace, no limit to God's love, and no limit to what God can do in us and through us. Thus, there is no limit to our forgiveness of others.

When I was a child, a tragedy occurred on my mother's side of the family. One of my mom's sisters was involved in an auto accident. My aunt and her daughter were together when they saw my uncle in a nearby car with another woman. My uncle tried to flee to protect the identity of the other woman. Therefore, when my uncle saw an approaching train, he cut across the tracks just before it. Unfortunately, my aunt was so focused on catching my uncle that she never saw the oncoming train. As a result, she crashed into the locomotive. My aunt died several days later, but my cousin survived and told the story.

After my aunt's death, my uncle went to his wife's siblings to seek their forgiveness. Unfortunately, not all were willing to forgive him. One sister refused and said she would never forgive or forget that he had caused her sister's death. She also warned that she'd shoot him if he tried to approach her, seeking forgiveness.

Although my uncle knew about the warning, his need for forgiveness consumed him. Unfortunately, it also blinded him to the danger that awaited him.

When my uncle arrived at this aunt's home, he found her standing on her front porch with a shotgun in her hand. The moment he stepped out of his car, he heard the words, "You take one more step toward this house, and you will be a dead man." Despite his tears and expression of sorrow and repentance for what he had done, his sister-in-law would have none of it. So he left with the past still very much a part of his present.

Although the other siblings tried to reconcile their sister with their brother-in-law, no progress was ever made until the night my aunt was lying in a hospital bed. Then, our pastor, in the presence of other family members, shared the gospel with her. That night, my aunt gave her life to Christ and received Him as Lord and Savior. Those who were with her said the first words she spoke following her conversion were, "get John (not his real name), her brother-in-law, and bring him to me. I want to tell him I love him and forgive him."

Within 30 minutes, my uncle arrived and was met with outstretched arms instead of a loaded shotgun. There were tears and hugs, but most of all, there was the light of Christ in my aunt's life. When she received Christ, she received His ability and power to forgive and love others, including her enemy. She recovered from her illness and continued living in such a way that her forgiving spirit and love for God gave convincing evidence of her salvation.

Humility

> Without humility, we cannot learn from others, we will not submit to others, and we will have difficulty turning to others in time of need.

Meekness is an essential aspect of the fruit of the spirit. The Greek word from which we get the word "meekness" also implies the idea of humility. Humility is the ability to be honest about our ability, or lack thereof. It is vital if we are to be teachable. The word *disciple* means to be a learner. Without humility, we cannot be a disciple, a follower of Christ. The apostle Peter was known for being arrogant and a know-it-all, but later, he displayed the value of humility.

> Likewise, you who are younger, be subject to the elders. Clothe yourselves, all of you, with humility toward one another, for 'God opposes the proud but gives grace to the humble.' 6 Humble yourselves, therefore, under the mighty hand of God so that at the proper time he may

exalt you, 7 casting all your anxieties on him, because he cares for you. (1 Peter 5:5-7)

Without humility, we cannot learn from others, submit to others, and have difficulty turning to others in times of need. But if Christ is in us, we have His Spirit of humility. Christ came into Jerusalem as a humble king, and when we receive Him as Lord and Savior, we take on His humble Spirit. Those who walk in humility have the assurance that the humble King lives within them and heaven awaits them.

"Say to the daughter of Zion, 'Behold, your king is coming to you, humble, and mounted on a donkey, and on a colt, the foal of a beast of burden '" (Matthew 21:5).

Love

The fruit of the spirit also includes love. God is love, and if God is in us, the love of God is in us. It means there will be a love for God and others that will permeate our souls. All true Christians have the spirit of Christ—the spirit of love in them.

We see the importance of love in Christ's Great Commandment statement. He tells us that all the laws and writings of the prophets are summed up in this commandment.

And he said to Him, 'You shall love the Lord your God with all your heart and with all your soul and with all your mind. 38 This is the great and first commandment. 39 And a second is like it: You shall love your neighbor as yourself.'

40 On these two commandments depend all the
Law and the Prophets." (Matthew 22:37-40)

> Our love for God, the things of God, and people
> provide evidence that we are children of God.

A Christ-follower is to love God the way Jesus loved His
Father. But a believer's love will not stop with loving God. It
will love others. Our love for God, the things of God, and
people provide evidence that we are children of God.

A believer should never think or say something like, "Well,
if they'd done to you what they did to me, you'd feel the same
way, and you wouldn't be able to forgive or love them either."
If one acts in this way, it tells us more about the unforgiving
person than about the one who needs forgiveness. It tells us that
the person is out of God's will or not a part of God's family.
"Beloved, let us love one another, for love is from God, and
whoever loves has been born of God and knows God. 8 Anyone
who does not love does not know God, because God is love" (1
John 4:7-8).

The love that Jesus and John refer to is not just any kind of
love. It is both a noun (a feeling) and a verb (an action kind of
love). It's a love that cares about the needs of others and will
sacrifice to meet those needs. It gives the thirsty a cup of cold
water, helps clothe the naked, and visits the sick (see Matthew
25:37-40). If God is in us, His love should flow from us.

In the Sermon on the Mount, Jesus stressed that His love differs from the world's idea of love. It's unconditional. He said:

> You have heard that it was said, 'You shall love your neighbor and hate your enemy.' [44]But I say to you, Love your enemies and pray for those who persecute you, [45]so that you may be sons of your Father who is in heaven. For he makes his sun rise on the evil and on the good, and sends rain on the just and on the unjust. (Matthew 5:43-45)

Loving your enemies, those who deliberately hurt you, is difficult, but it is possible, and it is necessary. Unfortunately, enemies can come from friends and family members. Who hasn't been hurt, intentionally or unintentionally, by someone on the job, at home, or in the church? Although we can't make others behave rightly, we can love rightly. If we love as Christ loved, we give evidence of our salvation. The more difficult a person is to love, the more they need our love. The more love we give them, the greater the evidence of Christ's power and love within us.

Several years ago, I had someone come by my office. This person had a list of complaints. Imbedded in the complaints were many personal criticisms meant to cause me pain. After two hours, the person left me with a more significant problem than a bruised ego. How would I be able to feel good about this person? It has never been my nature to strike out or want to get even, but I suddenly realized I had a problem. How would I be able to feel genuine love toward this person? I could treat him right; this, I was sure. I wouldn't have a problem being there in his time of need, but how could I feel good about him and look forward to being around him?

> Loving others unconditionally is not always easy, but it is possible. We may have to fast and pray, but we can do it.

I went to the altar and poured my heart out to God. I wanted to love this person the way Christ commands that I should love him and the way Christ loves him. The more I prayed, the more Christ filled me with His love and compassion. The Holy Spirit also reminded me during my prayer of something I had read. *People who hurt people are usually hurting people.*

When I finished praying, I felt love for this person. But I didn't stop there. I called a long-time member and asked if he knew anything about this person's childhood (I didn't share why I was asking). He said the person had experienced a very troubling and painful childhood. With this information, a greater sense of love and compassion for the person came over me.

Loving others unconditionally is not always easy, but it is possible. We may have to fast and pray, but we can do it. We have the power to love and forgive others because Christ lives within us. Our ability to love the unlovable gives us confidence that we truly belong to the God of love.

Righteousness

Christians are not perfect, but we do practice righteousness. Christians genuinely seek to obey God's commands. No other evidence stands out more in our day of immoral lifestyles and anti-absolute truth-thinking. Holy living cannot be an option for the believer; it must be a way of life. We are to be holy because God is holy. "But as he who called you is holy, you also be holy in all your conduct, 16 since it is written, 'You shall be holy, for I am holy '" (1 Peter 1:15-16).

The writer of Hebrews states that holiness is essential, "Strive for peace with everyone, and for the holiness without which no one will see the Lord" (Hebrews 12:14).

The apostle John confirms that those made righteous by Christ will live righteously for Christ. "If you know that he is righteous, you may be sure that everyone who practices righteousness has been born of him" (1 John 2:29). "No one born of God makes a practice of sinning, for God's seed abides in him, and he cannot keep on sinning because he has been born of God" (1 John 3:9). "We know that everyone who has been born of God does not keep on sinning, but he who was born of God protects him, and the evil one does not touch him" (1 John 5:18).

Unfortunately, the spiritual fog that fills our land has caused some to see grace as a license to sin. When this happens, God's grace is replaced with cheap grace—a grace that doesn't require holiness and doesn't produce thankfulness. Under the guise of this grace, many legitimize and excuse sinful actions and attitudes. They justify themselves by carefully selecting Bible verses while ignoring the context of the whole Bible, especially any verses on holiness and righteousness. Such actions turn God's amazing grace into a corrupt grace, which is not God's grace at all.

When God calls us into a saving relationship with His Son, He also calls us out of the world. Therefore, we are to reject lifestyles or actions contrary to the clear teachings of the Word of God.

The apostle Paul stresses the necessity of living a holy life. He writes:

> For at one time you were darkness, but now you are light in the Lord. Walk as children of light 9(for the fruit of light is found in all that is good and right and true), 10and try to discern what is pleasing to the Lord. 11Take no part in the unfruitful works of darkness, but instead expose them. 12For it is shameful even to speak of the things that they do in secret. (Ephesians 4:8-12)

Paul says that they were in darkness at some point, but not any longer. Therefore, as children of light, they must walk according to the light. They should no longer take part in the unfruitful works of darkness but expose them for all to see.

The apostle Peter also acknowledges the need for holiness. He writes:

But you are a chosen race, a royal priesthood, a holy nation, a people for his own possession, that you may proclaim the excellencies of him who called you out of darkness into his marvelous light. [10]Once you were not a people, but now you are God's people; once you had not received mercy, but now you have received mercy. [11]Beloved, I urge you as sojourners and exiles to abstain from the passions of the flesh, which wage war against your soul. (1 Peter 2:9-11)

The body of Christ is a holy nation that has been called out of the darkness and into His marvelous light. Therefore, we are to abstain from the works of darkness. We are to do battle against them, not surrender to them. We may lose some struggles along the way, but we will continue in the fight and win the war because we have the Commander of the Lord's army, Christ, with us and in us.

Just as salt makes us thirsty, receiving Christ gives us a desire for holiness and righteousness. Our hunger and thirst for holiness give us one more piece of convincing evidence of our salvation. Those who excuse sinful attitudes and actions under the guise of grace reveal a different salvation, a counterfeit one. "Blessed are those who hunger and thirst for righteousness, for they shall be satisfied" (Matthew 5:6).

Conviction/Confession

Although the convicting power of the Holy Spirit is not a fruit of the spirit, it is a compelling piece of evidence. When we sin, the Spirit convicts us. He may employ various means to bring this about. He may do it directly through our conscience, or He may send someone to speak to us. However, the most common method is reading, teaching, or preaching God's Word. A lack of conviction and a stubborn desire to continue living contrary to the clear instructions of God's Word show a rebellious or unregenerate state.

The convicting work of the Holy Spirit, combined with the humble spirit of a believer, will produce confession and repentance. Biblical Christians are not without sin, but they are sensitive to the Spirit's leading. When the Holy Spirit convicts us of a wrong that we've committed, and we confess and repent of it, we have substantial evidence of our salvation.

> If we experience these effects of salvation and witness the evidence of it, we can have the assurance we need.

The apostle John stresses the need for Christians to confess and repent of their sins. He writes:

> If we say we have no sin, we deceive ourselves, and the truth is not in us. 9 If we confess our sins, he is faithful and just to forgive us our sins and to cleanse us from all unrighteousness. 10 If we

say we have not sinned, we make him a liar, and
his word is not in us. (1 John 1:8-10)

In this verse, the Greek word translated in our English Bibles as
"to confess" comes from a Greek compound word that means *to
say/the same thing*. When we confess, we say the same thing
that God says about our actions or thoughts, in that they are
sinful. When we repent, we show our love for Him and
commitment to Him.

If we experience these effects of salvation and witness its
evidence, we can have the assurance we need. We can also have
confidence in the promises of God.

Chapter 11:
The Precious Promises

> If we have convincing evidence of our salvation, we can have confidence in God's promises.

Spiritual fog can cause people to believe that God will make us healthy, wealthy, and wise. But as the fog lifts, reality sets in. We suddenly discover that the Christian faith doesn't exempt us from evil people, tragic events, illnesses, and sorrows.

It doesn't exempt us, but it does provide for us. Christians are not given a free pass in this life, but we are given precious promises for this life. God's promises are essential to a life of faith. His promises are like anchors to a ship and a foundation to a building.

One of my Bible college professors said there are 7,474 promises in the Bible. Although some are specific to the Jewish people, many are for Christians.

If we have convincing evidence of our salvation, we can have confidence in God's promises. His promises are medicine to our soul and strength to our bones. They comfort us in pain and turmoil and encourage us in dark and discouraging times. I have called them salvation promises because they only apply to those who have truly experienced God's salvation.

These promises not only provide us with comfort and encouragement, but they also aid and strengthen our faith. What

I mean is that when we trust in God's promises and see God fulfill them, we are encouraged, and our faith is strengthened.

Some claim that biblical promises are nothing more than pie-in-the-sky stuff for those who have difficulty handling life. It would be true if they were not made by God, who has all power in heaven and earth. Promises are only as good as the ones making them. All biblical promises are like money in the bank. Although all of God's promises are important, I've only included a few I consider essential for the Christian life and have been instrumental in my own life. The first such promise is that of His presence.

His Presence

Unfortunately, Christians are victimized by criminals, laid off from work, injured in accidents, develop heart disease and cancer, and die way too young. In addition, Christians are often targeted, persecuted, and killed for their beliefs. The further our nation travels down the road of immorality, the more difficult and costly it will become for anyone who takes a stand for God and morality. Churches will face the loss of their non-tax status, and Christian business owners will face closing their doors or compromising their beliefs and practices. Unfortunately, only those ignorant of church history will be shocked by the persecution when it arrives.

A look back reveals such persecution during the early years of Christianity. Moreover, Paul and Peter's writings often encouraged those experiencing persecution by the Roman and Jewish segments of society.

> Without the presence of Christ, we will crumble and cave in, to the social, political, and judicial activism that seeks to rehabilitate us, indoctrinate us, and conform us to the ways of the world.

Before and during World War II, German churches faced compromising their biblical principles to conform to Hitler's and his Third Reich's version of morality or suffer the consequences. Likewise, in America, we are being pressured to conform to the ethics, or lack of, that is dictated by specific segments of society and canonized by the Supreme Court, or suffer the consequences.

Without the presence of Christ, we will crumble and cave-in, to the social, political, and judicial activism that seeks to rehabilitate us, indoctrinate us, and conform us to the ways of the world. But if God is for us and with us, who can be against us. The presence of God does more than comfort us. It empowers us. It encourages us. It enables us to stand firm when others are folding. Those who live in His presence can't be bought off, scared off, or bullied into submission.

> Keep your life free from love of money, and be content with what you have, for he has said, 'I will never leave you nor forsake you.' 6 So we can confidently say, 'The Lord is my helper; I

will not fear; what can man do to me?' (Hebrews 13:5-6)

> His presence not only comforts us but also encourages us, and strengthens us.

His presence is essential for the Christian life. But how is it made real in a believer's life? The promise of His company is the key. Our faith in God, combined with the work of the Holy Spirit, brings life and reality to His promises. It is essential because it's the reality of His presence that gives us confidence that every promise of God will be fulfilled. "You make known to me the path of life; in your presence there is fullness of joy; at your right hand are pleasures forevermore" (Psalm 16:11).

His presence not only comforts us but also encourages us and strengthens us. Although God exists outside the laws and realities of this world, He's able to make His presence a reality among us and in us? I've experienced it many times and. And sometimes, it can be overwhelming.

Before answering the call into the ministry, I worked at a coal-fired power plant. As part of my job requirement, I was stationed at different points in the plant from week to week. As a result, I sometimes found myself stationed in the basement of one unit shut down for a maintenance outage. An outage could last a week or many weeks. Sometimes, as on one particular night, there were very few people around and not much to do.

There were few routine tasks, but my main job was to wait for my supervisor to call on me to perform a specific task.

When stationed in the basement, we would operate out of a goat shack. It was a small shack like-structure approximately 6ft. X 6ft. When all my routine tasks were completed, and there was nothing else to do, I'd get my Bible out and read. But on this night, something strange happened. As I immersed myself in the Bible, I sensed a presence in the shack with me. I raised my eyes and looked all around but saw no one. As I continued reading, the presence became so strong that it was frightening. At one point, I jumped up and ran from the shack. This event took place during the two-year span in which I struggled with what I believed was a call of God to become a minister.

I genuinely believe that He will make himself real to us if we seek God. When He does, we must be ready to recognize Him (sometimes we don't.). Why is His presence so significant? Sometimes we know what action we need to take. We see the direction we need to go. We see the sin we need to confess. However, our problem is a lack of courage. We fear the consequences of taking that step, making that decision, and heading off in a different direction. In times like these, we need God's presence to be real to us. It is difficult to trust God, apart from God's presence. We need His presence.

In China, thousands of house churches meet regularly despite the constant threat of arrest and imprisonment. What gives them the courage and faith to defy the local authorities and be willing to suffer the consequences if caught? His presence!

One of His promises confirms this. Jesus promised to manifest His presence among those who come together for worship in His name. If they come together in His name, meaning the purpose for coming together is to honor and obey Him. In that case, Christ promises to make His presence real to them. He says this in Matthew 18:20, "For where two or three are gathered in my name, there am I among them."

His presence is not only vital to us; nothing can take it from us. Neither dictator, disease, or death can marginalize it, nix it, or remove it. Moreover, his presence is essential for confidence in all His other promises, such as the promise of His peace.

His Peace

God has given us the promise of His peace, but we only find it in Him. It's not found in self-help books, government programs or subsidies, or robust economic times. Instead, he promises us peace if we will make Him Lord of our lives and the focus of our minds.

His peace doesn't automatically happen because we have made Christ Lord and Savior. The key is having Him as our focus. We must center our lives and minds on Him. According to Isaiah, experiencing His peace depends on trusting God and staying focused on Him. "You keep him in perfect peace whose mind is stayed on you, because he trusts in you" (Isaiah 26:3).

According to Jesus, this peace requires a connection to Him. "I have said these things to you, that in me you may have peace. In the world, you will have tribulation. But take heart; I have overcome the world" (John 16:33).

I discovered that the peace Christ is referring to requires His presence. His presence must be real if His peace is to fill us. It is the promise of His presence that makes His peace a reality. This truth became real to me in the early 1980s when I was in a student training program at the fossil-fired power plant I mentioned earlier. Occasionally, the students were taken out of class to perform some less than desirable tasks, such as cleaning the black gooey sludge out of an oil tank of a large water pump. When that day came, I discovered I was claustrophobic.

Entering the tank required slithering one's way through a maze of pipes and tubes. The lone light bulb hanging from the opening on top still left the tank dark and foreboding. The door I entered was about two by three feet, and the tank itself was about seven feet wide, five feet long, and five feet high. The pipes, tubes, and oil pump made it seem smaller.

When I reached the bottom, I began having difficulty breathing. I looked up at the opening and then the walls of the tank. Fear gripped me as the impossible confronted me. The door shrank, and the walls began closing in on me. I realized that in a matter of minutes, I would be crushed. I closed my eyes and rehearsed in my mind, *This isn't happening—solid steel walls don't move, and steel openings don't shrink.* But when I

> The walls were closing in, and the door would soon be too small for an escape. If I didn't act quickly, this dark slimy tank would be my steel coffin, or so I thought.

once again opened my eyes, the impossible continued. The walls were closing in, and the door would soon be too small for an escape. If I didn't act quickly, this dark slimy tank would be my steel coffin, or so I thought.

Although things were not very clear to me, I distinctly remember three things that occurred almost simultaneously. First, I had reached the point that I was about to pass out (because of hyperventilation). Second, I was about to lose it emotionally and mentally and begin screaming for help. However, at that moment, a third thing occurred. A thought popped into my head from the Scriptures or rather a Bible verse. "I will never leave you nor forsake you" (Hebrews 13:5). I didn't know its reference, but I knew its truth. It was the words of Jesus. It was the words I needed. It was my lifeline to sanity. My fear had distracted me from God, but that verse reminded me of God. So, not one millisecond too soon, I closed my eyes and prayed.

As I prayed, God's presence became real to me. My breathing slowed, and my fears faded. When I finished my prayer, I forced one eye open, and to my delight, the tank had returned to normal. As I cleaned the tank, I rejoiced. I had discovered how to defeat an uncontrollable fear. Such power doesn't come from within us or from some self-help book that's been given to us. A belief in a higher power or an attempt to channel our spiritual energies (whatever that means) is not the answer to our fears. Jesus is the answer. His peace can conquer our fears, but His peace is found in His presence.

His Power

Salvation comes with the promise of His power. Many of His commands would be impossible to obey if not for His strength. His presence and power are necessary to accomplish His will. We see this in His command to evangelize:

> And Jesus came and said to them, 'All authority in heaven and on earth has been given to me. 19 Go therefore and make disciples of all nations, baptizing them in the name of the Father and of the Son and of the Holy Spirit, 20 teaching them to observe all that I have commanded you. And behold, I am with you always, to the end of the age. (Matthew 28:18-20)

He has all power and authority and has promised never to leave us; therefore, we can accomplish His will by accessing His power. It is the same power that raised Jesus from the grave.

> And what is the immeasurable greatness of his power toward us who believe, according to the working of his great might 20 that he worked in Christ when he raised him from the dead and

If we are to be more than conquerors through Christ, we must remember His power and tap into it.

seated him at his right hand in the heavenly
places. (Ephesians 1:19-20)

His power is good news, for it enables us to obey His Word.
It also means that if there's a will to obey, there is a way to
obey. God's power allows Christians to be free of sin's grip and
Satan's bondage. We don't have to live in bondage to our
emotions, powerful addictions, or anti-biblical lifestyles.
Instead, we can overcome fear, insecurities, and uncertainties.
If we are to be more than conquerors through Christ, we must
remember His power and tap into it. "No, in all these things we
are more than conquerors through him who loved us" (Romans
8:37).

However, just like the promise of His peace, His power is
connected to His presence. Paul said in his letter to the Philippi
Christians, "I can do all things through him who strengthens
me" (Philippians 4:13). Christ does not provide this power
apart from Himself; we must access it through Him. His
presence is necessary for His strength to be ours.

A friend shared with me a story told by William Curry, a
former NFL football player and college coach. Mr. Curry said
that when the Green Bay Packers drafted him, he was beaten
and bashed around by the other players during practice. It
reached the point that he was losing hope of making the team.
After practice one night, he was heading for his car when there
was a noise behind him. He thought it was some players who
didn't like him coming after him. He feared they were coming
to beat him up to get him to quit the team. He said he just sat
down on the grass and waited for what was about to happen, but

when he looked up, there was Willie Davis, who's now in the NFL hall of fame. When Mr. Curry told Willie that he didn't think he could stick it out. This big defensive lineman encouraged him, saying, "When you feel weak or unsure of yourself, look into my eyes and draw strength from me and then do what you need to do on that field." William Curry said, "From that moment on, I drew strength from my friend Willie."

We can't look into the eyes of our friend, Jesus, but we can fix our eyes on His promises and draw the strength we need for the battles we face. Although we may not see Jesus beside us, we can focus on His promise to be with us and know that He is there by faith.

> We can't look into the eyes of our friend, Jesus, but we can fix our eyes on His promises and draw the strength we need for the battles we face.

His Protection

As children of God, we have the promise of His protection. He is the Good Shepherd who watches over His sheep. He is our refuge in times of trouble. Jesus said, "I am the good shepherd. The good shepherd lays down his life for the sheep" (John 10:11). King David wrote, "In peace I will both lie down and sleep; for you alone, O Lord, make me dwell in safety" (Psalm 4:8). And the sons of Korah wrote:

1God is our refuge and strength,
    a very present help in trouble.
2Therefore we will not fear though the earth gives
        way,
    though the mountains be moved into the
        heart of the sea,
3though its waters roar and foam,
      though the mountains tremble at its
      swelling. Selah

(Psalm 46:1-3)

God said through the prophet Isaiah:

> No weapon that is fashioned against you shall succeed, and you shall confute every tongue that rises against you in judgment. This is the heritage of the servants of the Lord and their vindication from me, declares the Lord. (Isaiah 54:17)

Our enemies may plot and plan, and Satan may stretch out his hand, but God has promised His protection.

Our enemies may plot and plan, and Satan may stretch out his hand, but God has promised His protection. We are safe in the arms of Jesus and under His watchful eye. So when the enemy approaches, fix your eyes on His promises, believe in His love, and trust His power.

I've always been an insecure person. I often wonder why God has called me into the ministry. I'm no fighter, nor am I a walking bundle of confidence, but what I do have going for me are God and His promises. I am constantly amazed at the confidence and security that His promises give me. When pastors have disgruntled members confront us, falsely accuse us, or threaten to see us removed from the pulpit, the Word of God is there to reassure us. The same is true for believers in the workplace. You don't have to fear the boss or the company who threatens you with demotions or firings for refusing to obey orders, which are contrary to God's will and Word.

Those walking in His will can trust in His promised protection. The apostle Paul understood this. It's why he didn't fear men or governments. He knew God would protect him until his mission was completed. And when he realized God was finished with him, he wrote:

> For I am already being poured out as a drink offering, and the time of my departure has come. 7 I have fought the good fight, I have finished the race, I have kept the faith. 8 Henceforth there is laid up for me the crown of righteousness, which the Lord, the righteous judge, will award to me on that Day, and not only to me but also to all who have loved his appearing. (2 Timothy 4:6-8)

We can fight the good fight, finish the race, and keep the faith because we have the promise of His protection through it all.

As we focus on God's presence and trust in His promises, our fears and worries dissipate like fog under the morning sun. He also promises to provide for us.

His Provision

Christians have the promise of God's provisions. We may not know how He will do it or when He will do it, but we have the assurance that He will do it. He may give us a job opportunity or an unexpected check in the mail. He may guide an individual to help us or provide a ministry that reaches out to us. When in need, we can turn to His promises. So knowing His promises is crucial, trusting in them is a must, and crying out to Him is a necessity if we want Him to provide for us. "For he delivers the needy when he calls, the poor and him who has no helper" (Psalm 72:12).

Jesus put it this way:

> And I tell you, ask, and it will be given to you; seek, and you will find; knock, and it will be opened to you. 10 For everyone who asks receives, and the one who seeks finds, and to the one who knocks it will be opened. 11 What father among you, if his son asks for a fish, will instead of a fish give him a serpent; 12 or if he asks for an egg, will give him a scorpion? 13 If

you then, who are evil, know how to give good gifts to your children, how much more will the heavenly Father give the Holy Spirit to those who ask him! (Luke 11:9-13)

God provided His people with manna in the mornings and quail at night during their 40-year journey in the wilderness. God first used a brook and ravens to take care of Elijah and then a widow and her son (see 1 Kings 17:1-16).

God promises to provide for us. Just as loving fathers delight in meeting the needs of their children, God enjoys meeting our needs. We have a wonderful relationship with God through His Son, Jesus Christ. We have 24/7 access to our heavenly Father through prayer. We can confidently bring our needs to Him. Through Christ, we have all we need. We have an all-powerful God who cares for us and reassures us with His promises. "Casting all your anxieties on him, because he cares for you" (1 Peter 5:7).

And my God will supply every need of yours according to his riches in glory in Christ Jesus. 20To our God and Father be glory forever and ever. Amen." (Philippians 4:19-20)

Besides all His promises for this life, He has promised us a place beyond this life.

> We have a promise that when life turns against us, friends forsake us, family members disown us, illness consumes us, and our future fades before us, we have a home awaiting us.

His Place

Jesus has promised to take us home to His place. The moment we are saved, we are provided with the hope of a heavenly home. But, unfortunately, this world is not our home. The good news of the gospel ends with the grand home of heaven. When life turns against us, friends forsake us, our family disowns us, illness consumes us, and our future fades before us, we have a home awaiting us.

Jesus said:

> Let not your hearts be troubled. Believe in God; believe also in me. 2 In my Father's house are many rooms. If it were not so, would I have told you that I go to prepare a place for you? 3 And if I go and prepare a place for you, I will come again and will take you to myself, that where I am you may be also. (John 14:1-3)

When I was in Bible College, I heard about a pastor from a communist country who shared some events during his ministry. At one point, he was arrested, beaten, and threatened with death if he didn't reveal the names of pastors and the locations of the underground churches.

The police captain in charge of the interrogation said to him, "Do you not understand that I have the power to put you to death if you do not cooperate?"

The pastor then replied, "Do you understand what happens to a believer when he dies? Upon his death, he goes immediately into heaven and the presence and glory of the Lord. So you're threatening me with glory. The threat of glory will not make me talk." After some more threats, he was released. The promise of heaven takes away the fear of death and its power over us.

Some say, *There's no place like home.* It is even truer when heaven is our home. The apostle John tried to explain it in terms that would give us a glimpse of its beauty and majesty. So it is only fitting that God's Word closes with a description of our heavenly home. He writes:

> The wall was built of jasper, while the city was pure gold, clear as glass. [19]The foundations of the wall of the city were adorned with every kind of jewel. The first was jasper, the second sapphire, the third agate, the fourth emerald, [20]the fifth onyx, the sixth carnelian, the seventh chrysolite, the eighth beryl, the ninth topaz, the tenth chrysoprase, the eleventh

> jacinth, the twelfth amethyst. [21]And the twelve
> gates were twelve pearls, each of the gates made
> of a single pearl, and the street of the city was
> pure gold, transparent as glass. (Revelation
> 21:18-21)

John used the most precious materials of this world to paint a picture of the wonder and beauty of our future home. While we are in these fleshy bodies and live in this material-focused world, things such as pearls and gold hold great value to us. But once we are transformed and receive our glorified bodies, the things we treasure most will not be the streets of gold or the gates of pearl, but the Son of God.

Heaven will be a glorious place because the glory of the Lord will fill it, and we will dwell in it forever.

May we treasure the promise of heaven, a promise we can trust in, a guarantee of dwelling in an eternal home with Christ forever and ever. It's a promise worth taking to the grave.

Conclusion

Life is a journey. It began the day we were born, but it will not end when we die. Just as we did not cease to exist when we moved out of the house we were raised in, neither will we cease to exist the day we move out of the body in which we dwell. Therefore, our spiritual journey is so important. Our journey in this life will determine the direction of our journey beyond this life. And the key to making the right choices, traveling the right path, and arriving at the desired destination is truth. Therefore, seeking truth, being open to truth, and receiving and acting on truth is vital to a journey well-traveled.

The Bible says in Acts 17:11 that the people of Berea "received the word with all eagerness, examining the Scriptures daily to see if these things were so."

The biblical truths we need are found in the Bible we have. However, truth in a book is just words on a page. The power of truth is realized when it is received into your mind and heart and embraced as a manual for life and death.

My book helps you to search the Scriptures, especially those that address the subjects of spirituality, salvation, and eternal life. However, it only touches the surface of God's Word. Therefore, I encourage you to get into the Bible and search for yourself what it says about God, Jesus, and eternal life. In it, you will find the way to God, the Son of God, and the hope that only God gives.

And this is the testimony, that God gave us eternal life, and this life is in his Son. [12]Whoever has the Son has life; whoever does not have the Son of God does not have life." (1 John 5:11-12)

"I love those who love me, and those who seek me diligently find me" (Proverbs 8:17).

God has our journey laid out for us, but we must embrace it. God's promise to Israel is true for us, as well:

For I know the plans I have for you, declares the Lord, plans for welfare and not for evil, to give you a future and a hope. 12 Then you will call upon me and come and pray to me, and I will hear you. 13 You will seek me and find me, when you seek me with all your heart. (Jeremiah 29:11-13)

Jesus uses the word "come" instead of "seek."

Come to me, all who labor and are heavy laden, and I will give you rest. [29]Take my yoke upon you, and learn from me, for I am gentle and lowly in heart, and you will find rest for your souls. [30]For my yoke is easy, and my burden is light. (Matthew 11:28-30)

Do you rest in the assurance that heaven awaits you? Are you sure you are traveling the right path? Is truth knocking at your door? Is God speaking to you? If so, you have three choices. You can ignore it. You can run from it. Or you can open the door of your mind and receive it. The choice is yours. You alone have the power to unlock the door of your heart and mind.

William Holman Hunt's famous painting shows Jesus preparing to knock on a long unopened door covered with vegetation overgrowth with no handle on the outside. Only you can open it. Listen closely. Read the Scriptures carefully. Is Jesus trying to get your attention? Is there some truth He wants you to receive? If so, don't let the weeds of unbelief and skepticism prevent you from responding to it. Listen to it, then open your mind and receive it.

My hope and prayer are that you will not let the spiritual fog that plagues this world keep you from the Savior who loves you, died for you, and provided a book of truth to guide you. Therefore, consider this: Eternity is too long, heaven is too magnificent, and you are too loved by God not to want the truth and nothing but the truth.

Are you sure you have been saved by the One who conquered death and awaits you in heaven? If not, then do whatever it takes to be sure. However, it simply comes down to trusting God and His Word, for everything else that one says about life, death, heaven, and everything in-between are just people's opinions.

> "I write these things to you who believe in the name of the Son of God, that you may know that you have eternal life." (1 John 5:13)

Endnotes

Chapter 2: The Deceptions Along the Way

1. Robert J. Morgan, On This Day, Nashville, Thomas Nelson Pub., March 15, 1997.

2. Hank Hanegraaff, Christianity In Crisis, Harvest House Pub., 1977, p. 10.

Chapter 3: The Shortcuts to Avoid

3. https://lifewayresearch.com/2007/08/07/reasons-18-to-22-year-olds-drop-out-of-church/

4. https://lifewayresearch.com/2020/09/08/americans-hold-complex-conflicting-religious-beliefs-according-to-latest-state-of-theology-study/

Chapter 5: The Self-Examination

5. John Telford, The Life of John Wesley, The Wesley Center Online, Chapter 6, Paragraph 7 & 8, http://wesley.nnu.edu/john-wesley/the-life-of-john-wesley-by-john-telford/

6. Ibid., chapter 7, paragraph 10

Chapter 6: The Right Path

7. Robert J. Morgan, How Firm a Foundation, Near to the Heart of God, Revell, 2010, p. June 8.

Chapter 8: The Spiritual Benefits

8. Robert J. Morgan, Then Sings My Soul, Thomas Nelson Pub., 2006, p. 421.

Scriptures Quoted and Referenced:

Genesis
1:1   90

Exodus
8:18   59
15:11   96

Numbers
16:1-23   110

I Samuel
12:20-23   138-139

1 Kings
17:1-16   181

Psalm
4:8   178
16:11   170
19:1   05
19:1-2   93
27:10   140
37:4   131
46:1-3   178
72:12   180
119:11   95

Proverbs
8:17   186

Isaiah
26:3   172
54:17   178

Jeremiah
17:9   129
24:7   131
29:11-13   186

Ezekiel
36:26-27   132

Jonah
1:1-5   58

Matthew
5:6   163
5:43-45   159
5:43-48   130
6:15   154
6:33   126
7:13-14   40, 102
7:26-27   122
8:19-20   08
9:12-13   98
11:28-30   186
18:20   172
18:21-22   154
19:27-29   103-104
21:5   157
22:36-40   111-112

22:37-40	157-158	Acts	
24:35	85	4:12	100
25:21	151, 157	17:11	49, 185
25:21, 23	97		
25:37-40	157-158	Romans	
28:18-20	175	1:20	93-94
		3:10-12	99
Mark		5:17	101
9:43-48	110-111	6:1-2	116
10:45	123	6:11-14, 22	117
		6:20-23	121
Luke		8:18	106, 144
11:9-13	180-181	8:29	147
16:13	120	8:37	176
19:10	90	12:2	118
John		1 Corinthians	
3:3-13	128	2:14	46
3:5	123	3:12	84
3:16	99	15:54-57	83
6:44	68		
8:32	01	2 Corinthians	
8:44	59	4:3-4	85
10:10	12, 82	5:17	113, 123
10:11	177	12:9-10	61
14:1-3	182	12:10	124-125
14:6	100	13:5	68, 153
14:16-18	133		
14:16, 26	25	Galatians	
15:19-20	08	5:22-23	153
16:7	25		
16:33	172	Ephesians	
17:12	70	1:19-20	175-176

2:1-3	145	James	
3:20-21	143-144	1:14-15	19, 20
4:4-6	147	2:8-10	112
4:8-12	162	4:7	12
4:20-24	149		
5:26	86	1 Peter	
6:12	02	1:3-4	138
		1:14-17	114
Philippians		1:15-16	161
3:13-14	135	1:23	128
4:6-7	143	2:2-3	60, 146
4:13	134, 176	2:9-11	163
4:19-20	181	3:18	101
		5:5-7	156-157
Colossians		5:7	181
1:19-20; 2:10	124		
		2 Peter	
2 Timothy		2:4	109
3:16-17	92	3:18	43
4:6-8	180		
		1 John	
Titus		1:8-10	164-165
3:5	127-128	2:29	161
		3:9	161
Hebrews		3:9; 4:7; 5:1	128
2:14-15	151-152	4:7-8	158
4:12-13	79	5:11-12	100, 186
10:24-25	148	5:13	81, 84, 188
12:14	161	5:18	161
13:5	174	5:19	11
13:5-6	169-170		
13:14	132	2 John	
		2:7	17

Jude
11   110

Revelation
4:8   96
12:9   17
21:1-4   139-140
21:18-21   183-184

CPSIA information can be obtained
at www.ICGtesting.com
Printed in the USA
BVHW081747090222
628492BV00010B/1240